How To

Brilliant Business Blogs

The no-bullsh*t guide to writing blogs that boost your brand, business and customer loyalty.

by

Suzan St Maur

*Jeannie is looking forward to spending your money!!...
With all good wishes
Suzan StMaur
June 2015.*

First Published in Great Britain 2014
by www.HowToWriteBetter.net

© Copyright Suzan St Maur

ISBN-13: 978-1500340612

ISBN-10: 1500340618

WHAT THE PRE-REVIEWERS SAID...

"I have been writing business blogs for my site for a couple of years now, and thought I had little left to learn. Although, being in a very niche market, it's very easy to run out of ideas of what to write about. When I started reading "How to Write Brilliant Business Blogs" I realised that there is much left for me to learn, and before long I had a pad and pencil at my side, writing down ideas as they occurred to me while reading this book. The pad is now full of new ideas, and I feel re-invigorated with enthusiasm about my blog. The book is written in a relaxed conversational style, and feels more like having a chat with a (very knowledgeable and experienced) friend rather than reading a book. The first part of the book sets the scene, and then there is a comprehensive A to Z section, making it easy to dip in and out of. I must confess I read the book from cover to cover as soon as I received it, but I know I shall be re-visiting it time and again to refresh my thinking and gain some new ideas. Whether you are a complete novice at blogging, or a seasoned professional, this book has much to offer, and I would highly recommend it."

Jane Hatton
Founder/Director
www.Evenbreak.co.uk

"Everyone who is contemplating a business blog needs to read this book. Not only does it take you step-by-step through everything you need to know about setting up your blog, it also enables you to manage the process so that you'll keep up the momentum and achieve your business aims. It contains easily digestible, bite sized chunks of sound advice on every aspect of business blogging. With this book in your armory, blogging stops being a looming chore and starts to be an inspiration-filled fun activity which will also drive revenues to your business."

Cathy Dobson

CEO

Red Door Consulting GmbH

Fantastic! At long last, some common sense writing about how businesses can use blogging effectively. I know I need to blog for my business but have shied away from it because I thought it would take a lot of time out of my otherwise very busy diary and that I didn't have the skill to create effective copy. This book not only has given me tools and an A-Z, literally, of blogging tips, but it has also given me confidence in that I already have the necessary tools to create an effective blog and that it doesn't take up anywhere near as much time as I thought it would. It's easy to follow steps, jargon busting techniques and putting things into plain English context, has meant that for the first time ever, I am now planning our first year's blogging campaign for our new business. Thank you Suze. ☺

Cindy-Michelle Waterfield

Co-Founder

Sales & Marketing Director

www.IWantASpeaker.com

"Getting the right tone has always been the hardest aspect of business blogging for me. Finding a unique voice which strikes the right balance between professional authority and a warm and personal style, appropriate to the audience, is the most challenging thing to get right, and Suzan's advice about what to consider is spot-on. A valuable toolkit for every business blogger"

Maya Middlemiss

Saros Research Ltd

www.sarosresearch.com

"Thanks so much for the opportunity to read your new book. I now feel much better equipped to develop our business blog. The first thing that I am about to do today is to develop our blogging strategy and thanks to you, I now have a basis on which to start. So thanks.

I would love to submit a review:"

"'What a wonderful resource, Suzan gives practical guidance firstly, how to develop a business blog strategy, then goes on to sourcing content and how to structure your writing. A wonderful and inspirational book for anyone considering entering the fun and rewarding business blogging arena.'"

"I wish you every success in the publication and promotion of your book, you deserve it."

Bryce Anderson

CEO - Light Degree Ltd

Job scheduling and CRM for field workers

www.lightdegree.com

"From one of the best and most experienced bloggers about writing, this book contains everything (that I can think of) you need to know about blogging for business. Suzan St Maur takes you through the step-by-step process of writing engaging blogs, and answers an A-Z of questions about how to attract readers, use your blog as part of your sales funnel, manage your SEO, and write on a variety of subjects from the personal to the professional. If you're a blogger, a business or a beginner, this book is one you can't afford not to read."

Lucy McCarraher
Managing Editor
Rethink Press
http://www.rethinkpress.com

"I have been a fan of Suzan St. Maur's work for a while now. So, when she asked me if I could review her latest release, I felt more than honored.

'How to Write Brilliant Business Blogs' is the best book on business blogging I have ever read. It offers gems on every page. And Suzan's usual writing style, wittiness, and gusto, which make her such a unique and endearing professional, also help drive the message home.

Like many, I don't have time for long spiels. I love organized content that allows for easy skimming. 'How to Write Brilliant Business Blogs' is perfect in that sense. From customer experience to grammar, headlines, humour, and social media sharing, Suzan covers in depth everything you need to know about blogging. She also provides specific examples and resources that even seasoned writers will find useful.

My favorite thing about this book? The inclusion of ideas for industries that don't get much coverage, such as gardening, used cars, bed & breakfasts, health and safety, insurances, and law.

I do not say this often but Suzan is a rare individual in her field. Not only does she deserve the title of expert, but she also has this uncanny ability to speak to you as if you were the only person in the room.

I recommend 'How to Write Brilliant Business Blogs' to anyone interested in taking their blog to the next level, no matter their what their experience level is currently."

Cendrine Marrouat
Social media coach, blogger, curator, journalist, and author
Winnipeg, Manitoba, Canada
www.socialmediaslant.com

"As a former teacher and someone who taught computer novices in the early 1980s (everyone was a beginner then!), I learned that people needed "baby" step instructions and Suzan's book is just that. She makes blogging easy and she takes what others have made complex and makes it simple. "

Trudy Van Buskirk
Marketing Guide and Storytelling Coach for Women
www.boomerbizbuilder.com

Whether you are a new blogger or you have years of experience behind you, How to Write Brilliant Business Blogs is a must-have. It's filled with relevant, straightforward information arranged in an easy-to-find format, making it an ideal reference for those middle-of-a-post questions. I will definitely be recommending this to my blogging clients.

Marie Leslie
Social Media, Marketing & Business Consultant
Marie Leslie Media
www.marieleslie.com

"I really liked this. Not only for the no nonsense approach so people can just get on with blogging and not bother overmuch with the deep theory of blogging, also liked the guidance on frequency and blogging types which makes it a lot clearer than around 99% of other stuff I have read. Really like it."

Sue Edwards
Law Hound Ltd
www.Lawhound.co.uk

Contents

INTRODUCTION

Hey – congratulations on your having joined the business blogosphere.

Happily this does not require you to practice giving a weird handshake or entering the room with a rolled up trouser/pants leg.

Blogging for business is simply another opportunity for you to market yourself and your business in a specific, and very useful way. Online.

No, it's nothing like advertising

Until quite recently many businesses saw blogging as another form of advertising.

But as I'm sure you know, not only has blogging changed: the whole marketing scene has changed completely, especially online.

I could go on for hours about the details but that's not what we're here to talk about in this book.

Basically though, blogging is part of a bloody great paradigm shift away from the days when you sold stuff to people in one-way communication, to a time now when you get involved with your marketplace, get to know the people, and then help them to buy.

Somebody the other day wrapped it up quite neatly when she said...

"People now don't want presentations.
They want conversations."

So how does blogging fit into this picture? Why has it become such a must-have element in your marketing?

Where blogging belongs in the "sales funnel"

Many experts will talk about the position of the company blog within the overall context of the **sales funnel**, and what it really boils down to is that the blog does two very important things for your business.

Number one, at the fat, top end of the sales funnel, is that it provides your prospects with the chance to get to know you and your brand at a personal level – and establish the groundwork for your relationship with them. It's all nice and relaxed, not at all pushy. This inspires confidence and trust, and helps make you and your brand likeable.

Never forget the fact that **people like to do business, with people they like**. Your blog is a highly valuable tool to build mutual admiration with prospects so they're then ready to move on into the next phase of the sales funnel.

Number two, at the thin, lower end of the sales funnel, is that your blog promotes an ongoing relationship with your actual customers or clients. It reassures them that you and your brand are not just some one-trick pony that takes their money and gallops off. It shows them that you're thinking of their needs, which reinforces their long-term loyalty.

Something else you should never forget…**it costs a lot more to win new business than it does to perpetuate business you already have**. Your blog is a highly valuable tool to help you keep and grow it.

And another very valuable point…

There's an additional issue that's being talked about at the time of writing (mid-2014) - another very good reason for never putting your blog aside in favor of social media communications, even by publishing articles and blog posts directly on to platforms like LinkedIn and Facebook.

This is the difference between "owned content" - your website, your blog and your email marketing, i.e. anything you publish yourself and control 100 percent - and anything you publish elsewhere.

Although the WWW started off as free and sharing of everything from the kindness of everyone's hearts, not surprisingly the big SocMed platforms have begun to tighten the screws down on monetization of their businesses so the freebies are drying up.

No longer can you count on posts you put up on your business page on Facebook being seen by all the page's followers; you're lucky if it gets transmitted to 20 of them. If you want more, you pay. Actually this is very good value for money because you can target your audience very carefully with little wastage, but that's not really what business blogging is about. Pay Per Click and online advertising, etc., are not the same as blogging.

Other platforms, as I write this, are probably licking their lips and dreaming up similar monetizing schemes to get bloggers putting their hands in their pockets just like advertisers do.

So hang on to your "owned content" and don't listen to people who tell you that blogging and email marketing are dead – they are immortal, because they are the only fast-moving online media you control totally.

This book is the one no-one else has got around to writing yet: not how to install widgets, but what to write about when the widgets and other toy-toys installed and working. I hope the book will give you plenty of "light bulb" moments and some great ideas for your business blogs.

 *from HowToWriteBetter.net (HTWB)*

Questions? Give me a shout on suze@suzanstmaur.com

SORTING OUT YOUR BLOGGING STRATEGY

I wish I had a dollar, pound, euro, rupee, or whatever currency you like for every time I see an article or blog post that goes into vast technical detail on how you should develop your blogging strategy.

OK, if you are Coca Cola or General Motors, this probably is something that you need to take seriously. But then if you are Coca Cola or General Motors your choices of staff toilet paper are likely to require lengthy policy documents that need to be peer-reviewed and ratified by anything up to Board level.

Yes, you need a blogging strategy. No, it does not need to be complex.

But, it's a good idea because it helps to stop you running out of steam.

First of all you need to take a good, long, hard look at your readers / clients / customers / prospects (as always) and think about the sort of information they will find useful. Yes, that one again. But I can't emphasize the importance of this too much: **it's essential.**

Now, before you start worrying about individual blog topics you could write to inform and entertain them, think first in terms of **blog post types** that you could use – then flesh those out into individual posts.

So for instance …

How-To blog posts … always popular although a wee bit overdone at times. However they're probably not overdone in your niche, so think in terms of all the functions and processes your audience might need to go through and run up a list of posts based on each one of those. And don't try to cram too much information into each one.

Remember that although people argue until they're blue in the face over how long a blog post should be, the answer is – OK – as long as it needs to be. But folks don't really want to read more than a few hundred words at a time. Space your how-to posts out into digestible chunks.

Lists … another almost-cliché in the blogosphere, but they still work. Numbers attract. Some of the woo-woo gurus even tell you what numbers readers will find attractive … 7, 10, but never 13 … etc. Whatever numbers you can muster, numbering your key points is attractive to blog traffic.

Tips … following on from lists and numbers, XX top tips on how to do whatever will get attention. These usually are easy to extract from your own written information, or from your brain when you're working through a process or other activity within your business.

Feature articles ... posts based on your own observations, ideas and thoughts relevant to your business and more importantly, those of your target audience.

Historical material ... why and how your business, and the businesses of your target audience, have come into being in the first place. These are more entertaining than they are informative in terms of contemporary information, but are nonetheless interesting and attractive.

And so-on.

Next, work out the frequency of your blogging

It's all very well to listen to the "gurus" who say you should blog 3 times per week, every day, or whatever.

However, what's important here is **what works for you**.

OK, a lot depends on your industry, your own business, and the relationship you have with your readers. (Notice I do *not* say how much time you have to spare ... that's not the right way to look at things if you want your blog to enhance your turnover and profits.)

Given the choice, I would say that regularity is more important than spontaneity. Your blog is your means of establishing worthwhile communication with your readers/customers/prospects, and they will come to appreciate a regular post from you whether – within reason – it's every day, once a month, or once a week.

If my back is up against the wall? I'll say go for once a week. That's a "do-able" amount for most business people and it's also a useful interval for communicating with your audience.

So, 52 or so posts a year?

Sounds like a lot, doesn't it? But look at it this way ... here are the main categories again, and on the once-a-week basis you only need to produce around 12 of each per year.

How-To blog posts ... surely you can think of 12 or more how-to posts about your business or activity that your readers will gobble up with interest?

Lists ... are a superb way to share information from your own skill set – or as a means of curating other blog posts which you admire. Number them and include the number in your headline (10 top tips to help you .....) because although I personally feel that approach is a bit of a cliché now – am I a snob or what? – numbers like that still draw attention when used in headlines.

Tips ... ditto. If and when you run out of your own tips and ideas, research your topic and share others' tips that you admire and feel are worth sharing with your own readers. Your recommending them won't cause you to lose credibility: on the contrary. Your readers will admire your perspicacity and generosity in sharing.

Feature articles ... given that events in your business – and those of your customers – are likely to be changing as rapidly as everything else, there shouldn't be a problem for you to find enough material. If you should find yourself short of ideas, look beyond your own immediate business and examine related issues that can affect your business and those of your readers. Given the speed at which business is churning and evolving, you shouldn't go short.

Historical material … having been born and grown up in the 20th century I still feel a bit offended when people talk about my childhood days as if those had been in the Ming Dynasty. No matter how young you are, never forget that some of your readers / customers may have been born before Prince's prophetic 1999. (Don't ya just love the music though? Check it out on YouTube!) And use historical information to underline your own in-depth knowledge of your business. When you start thinking about it, there are very few areas of business which do *not* have a history. Use them.

Editorial calendars

Editorial calendars do pretty much what the name suggests: they provide you with somewhere to set out your blogging (and other social media) plans for the upcoming weeks, months, and whole year.

Geekier readers might find their eyes lighting up when I say that there are vast numbers of digital editorial calendar devices you can download and install that will plan everything from a blog post once a week to an entire military invasion of the Moon. Just Google "editorial calendar" and watch what comes up.

Non-geeks can relax, however. Most DIY blog facilities (like WordPress) offer basic calendars to store drafts and schedule posts ahead of publication time, allowing you to move things around and plan ahead while leaving yourself some flexibility to add new things in at the last minute.

(And if you're really technophobic you can even use a paper-based calendar or print diary.)

So relax. Read this book, then work out what you're going to write about.

I'm so sorry to trivialize the advice you might be given by other blogging experts, but, it's that simple.

Unless you're running a mega-humungous corporation, your blogging policy needs only to consist of a) what you feel your audience will benefit from in terms of your contributions, and b) what you learn from your audience, on that they want to read about.

Yes, you could do well to structure a "blogging policy" that encompasses all these issues, especially if you have other people in your organization who will be contributing to your business blog, and incorporate all that into your "editorial calendar."

As long as everyone in your organization understands the above, your blogging strategy will work superbly.

THE BASICS OF SEARCH ENGINE OPTIMIZATION (SEO)

Please note that I am NOT an expert in SEO, so if you need and/or want to learn about it you need to read another book. There are several excellent publications out there but one I would recommend – and it's free – is **The Beginner's Guide To SEO**, from **Moz.com**:

http://moz.com/beginners-guide-to-seo

However here are a few thoughts about SEO which you may find useful in the meantime.

SEO changed quite a bit in 2012 and 2013 when Google thankfully moved its goalposts and began to favour "fresh, original content" over pure keyword usage. This meant that it was no longer OK to stuff your junky content full of keywords like an old chesterfield and get it into the Google top 10 that way.

Many SEO experts wrung their hands in despair but writers like me were thrilled. At long last sites that were "link farms" – thousands of words of pure bullsh*t purporting to be blog posts, full of keywords and links and less sense than a chimpanzee would compose on a typewriter – got thrown in the garbage where they belonged.

To illustrate my point, here is an excerpt from one of these so called "blogs" that was so hilarious I shared it with readers on HowToWriteBetter.net ...

The very best communication strategies speak details on five W's and one H – Why, What, Who, When, Where and How, and help you strategies communication with viewers, other stakeholders and your co-workers. They improve the entertaining communication, provide framework for determining activities that require outreach, consider prospective mail messages and followers, and create automobiles to produce details.

The very best communication strategies are designed to increase the distributed details and reduce misinterpretations. Communication strategies must take into account concept, viewers, prospective automobiles, options required and reviews systems as the best communication strategies are the designs for making an offer to notify and to be advised by the others. They can also confirm to be quite useful in speeding up quick details distribution in fast unfolding activities.

In circumstances, when issues are complicated or delicate, best communication strategies help you to systematize details and deal with the issues that may happen out of these issues. Best Communication Strategies let you avoid prospective uncertainty about difficult issues, as you technique in advance.

And no, I'm not offering any prizes for anyone correctly guessing what the keywords were...

Now that such keyword-stuffing has been outlawed, we still mustn't assume that keywords have disappeared altogether. They're still important, and here are some hints on how to put yours together...

Keywords

Everywhere you look in internet marketing circles there is advice on everything to do with keywords, apart from one rather basic thing: how to decide on what keywords to start working with. Why is it that so few experts can give you a simple answer here?

In my ignorance about so many grown-up aspects of inbound/content marketing I have spent the last few weeks asking a variety of experts this seemingly silly question. But try as I might to find a straight answer, very few were forthcoming. I either got the impression that the question was so silly as not to be worth answering, or that the expert concerned just didn't damned well know.

Er, what's a keyword? They're words and phrases you use to grab hold of readers on Google and other search facilities, and when you're blogging you need to insert those words and phrases in appropriate places in your blog, and when you're setting your blog up before you publish it.

Let's look at three typical types of post and how to start researching for keywords on each one:

1. **Informational blog posts**. This is where blog posts provide readers with useful information without trying to poke them into the next step of the buying process for which, clearly,

they're not yet ready. Examples include historical pieces, assessments of current needs within a given marketplace or area of operation, reassurance pieces to show how you and your business are the go-to experts in your field.

2. **Solution blog posts**. These are for readers who know they need to find a solution but need some help in how to choose which one. These readers will find product and service reviews and comparisons helpful, but again without your using a cattle prod to move them towards your own offerings.

3. **Product/service support blog posts**. These articles are very useful to amplify the product/service offerings on your website, to back them up, to offer tips and notions on how to make best use of them, how to integrate them successfully within the reader's overall activities, etc.

Much as the "experts" out there can guide you with your keywords once you have figured them out, they can't come up with the original words and phrases you need to start with. And in fairness, they're not clairvoyant: you are the person who knows your business – and your customers – best of all, so you're the best person to get the ball rolling.

You need to put yourself in your customers' and prospects' shoes, and work out what they will be searching for when they're looking for what you offer. Sometimes this is more obvious than others.
Here's how I see your keywords starting off before you begin the wider research exercise:

1.Informational blog posts need to have initial keywords that capture:

Your product or service - including some specific clarification – not just "dog groomer," but "specialist poodle groomer"

Interest factor – "poodle grooming worldwide," "how to be a poodle groomer"

More specific notions – "grooming poodles", "grooming poodle crosses," "grooming cockapoos," "grooming labradoodles," "grooming golden poos," "trimming poodles," "clipping poodles," etc.

Background posts – "history of poodles," "poodle crosses," "why dogs shed hair," etc.

2.Solution blog posts keywords need to focus in harder on:

Your expertise and cost-efficiency – "expert poodle groomer, "cheap poodle grooming," "best poodle groomer"

Failures elsewhere – "poodle grooming disasters," "poodle grooming problems" "groom my poodle myself"

What to look for – "poodle grooming services," "gentle poodle grooming," "dog-friendly poodle grooming"

3. Product/service support blog posts

Local emphasis - "poodle grooming in (TOWN)," "poodle grooming locally (TOWN)," "local poodle grooming (TOWN)"

Convenience emphasis – "quick poodle grooming," "poodle grooming 24/7?

Value emphasis – "cheapest poodle grooming," "value poodle grooming," " low-cost poodle grooming"

Check out your competitors

Once you have a good idea of the keywords your customers and prospects might use (as shown above), whack those into Google or similar search box and see what turns up.

If there is nothing much, go on to your competitors' sites and check out their text on the home page. There's a good chance that you'll pick up on the keywords/phrases they're using, if only because many businesses still overdo the keyword usage and you'll see numerous manifestations of their favourites.

Never fail to use your common sense and instincts

Figuring out the right keywords to incorporate into your blog posts is not rocket science. It's a lot more about common sense and the ability to put yourself into your customers' and prospects' shoes.

I know you're more than capable of doing that, so go ahead – become a customer and figure out what you would search for when checking out blogs of interest.

A few other ideas

Here's another very useful tool to help you find the right keywords for your blogs:

https://freekeywords.wordtracker.com/searches

You have to sign up but there's no cost involved, and it's almost as good as the Google Keyword tool which still exists but now is more complex to get hold of.

And here's another trick which is a bit of a cheat and hardly scientific, but does give you a rough indication of the value of keyword alternatives…

Google a few variants of what you have in mind and see which return the largest number of results.

Let's say your blog post is about handwriting: I just Googled that …

Searched handwriting – 7,400,00 results

Searched writing by hand – 596,000,000 results

Obviously "writing by hand" is more searched for, but there is more competition on Google! So add some longer/different keywords to go with it and refine your search that way.

Searched why clear handwriting is important – 12,200,000

Searched why it's important to write clearly when writing by hand – 170,000,000

Aha, that's interesting. You'll see from the way Google sets out the entries that what's grabbed it here are the words "write clearly." Let's double check:

*Searched **write clearly** – 568,000,000*

Bingo. Of course "write clearly" can apply to other interpretations. But on this basis you might find it helpful to use "writing by hand" and "write clearly" as two of your major keyword phrases.

For more about the intricacies of search and keywords, stay tuned to HowToWriteBetter.net and Blog Writing News, as I will be focusing on that aspect of blog writing in the coming months and attempting to keep us all up to date on how SEO is evolving.

Above all though, don't get carried away with SEO and let the tail wag the dog. Although in the past the nuts-and-bolts elements of SEO were very important, and they still are up to a point … **what matters most of all, by a long way, is that you produce high quality original content.**

INTRODUCTION TO CHOOSING BLOG POST TOPICS

Finding topics to write about in your business blog isn't always easy. However it is is very easy to fall back on the tried, tested and often boring approaches still advised by some so-called blogging experts. Here's how to approach your choice of topics in slightly more interesting and less hackneyed ways.

Although you may well want to make sure you have covered all the initial bases in your business - the most obvious topics that are of direct concern to you and your customers - it helps to enrich your content with more probing, deeper topics. How to think those up? Do a bit of role play.

Imagine you have a commercial transport company

You have a fleet of vans and trucks which transport your customers' goods over medium to long distances around the country.

To begin with you're likely to blog about the quality of your service, what to watch out for if customers consider using your competitors, how your service compares with those of others, what alternatives there are for transportation of goods and why they are inferior (of course!) etc.

Those are all fine and dandy but they are very strong on inward focus. Yes, your customers will be interested to read those posts because they have a need to use such transport services.

But what about your customers' other needs?

For example, how should they prepare their goods for transportation so they are as well protected as possible? Do they know how important it is for them to give you a detailed inventory of the goods being transported, so that your people will know how best to handle them en route? Do you know someone who is an expert packer whom you can interview for a blog post, sharing his/her expertise to help your customers pack properly?

Moving on, what advice do your customers give to *their* customers who receive the goods transported by you? Could you help your customers improve their own service by issuing better instructions for unpacking, goods inward handling, etc.?

And then what about stock control, plus even JIT and other production strategies that relate to goods outward and transportation? What tips could you get from external experts to advise your customers on how to improve these elements of their business?

Make your blog your customers' favorite point of reference

The whole point about this example above is to give you an idea of how to dig deeper into what you can blog about that will really resonate with your customers. You could apply this approach to almost any type of business, big or small.

If you have a hairdressing business, don't just blog about topics relating to your actual customer herself. She has a family. What advice can you give her about her children's hair? Head lice? Baby's first haircut? Hair care for the elderly? Nutrition for healthy hair? Choosing the right style to suit people's faces and shapes, whatever age they are? Why a hairstyle can look great on a friend but won't work for you?

If you have a software company, don't - ever - get carried away with all the features of your product: focus on what it does for your customers. But don't merely write about how it helps them. Think about what products or services they are offering to their own customers, and emphasize how your product helps them deliver a better service. If your product is used by a range of different industry types, write posts about each different type - customers in other types of business will still learn from this.

Creating really valuable business blog posts requires some creative thought and a bit of clever digging. You should find plenty of inspiration (and shovels for the digging) in this book!

BLOGGING DIRECT TO SOCIAL MEDIA PLATFORMS

Several of the main social media platforms now allow you to post blogs directly on there and bypass your own site altogether. So how do you benefit from this option?

On Facebook and Google Plus, these amount essentially to long ordinary posts on a timeline.

On **Facebook**, in addition to posting on your own timeline you also can post articles as "notes," and write "reviews," as well as write posts on the timelines of groups you belong to, and in theory at least, your friends' timelines.

On **Google Plus** you just write a long post on your timeline, or the timeline of a community you belong to (or a community of your own, naturally.)

LinkedIn is a bit different, in that to post actual articles on the main home page you need to be invited to take up (or apply for) the honor of being allowed to publish posts direct...! This gets your post into LinkedIn's relatively new melting pot called "Pulse." You can also post fairly lengthy text as updates on the home page and in groups you belong to.

And those are just the main platforms.

Next question: why should you post blogs to social media?

At first glance it may seem a bit pointless to blog on social media platforms when you've got a perfectly good blog of your own. But there are some benefits.

Here are some that I can see...

When you want to blog about something topical or transient. Anything that appears in the SocMed is going to have a very short shelf life, whereas you want your own blog content to be pretty well evergreen so it doesn't date, or at least doesn't date too fast. If something crops up in your business or industry that you want to comment on very quickly, to a large audience, putting up a post on the most appropriate SocMed platform will get you noticed without cluttering your own site with yesterday's news.

When others in your marketplace are busy talking about your topic. If you can see that something that affects you closely is "trending" on a SocMed platform, posting a blog about it right there, unfortunately, is a faster way of getting your point across than if you expect people to click on through to your own blog.

When you want to blog about something that doesn't fit in your own blog. This happens to me from time to time - I feel a burning need to shoot my mouth off about something that isn't connected with writing, so it doesn't fit with the remit of my site, HowToWriteBetter.net – but will fit within the broader remit of a social media platform like LinkedIn.

From a business point of view this can be helpful in that it shows your colleagues, clients, customers and other readers that you're on the ball about what's going on in your industry, but respect the particular nature of your own blog and its readers so don't clutter it up with off-topic posts.

And when/why you shouldn't publish blogs to social media?

This has a lot to do with bringing your audience back home to Mama (or Papa.) Much as internet-wide discussions are commonplace now, there comes a time when you need to be a little less public-spirited and a little more commercial.

By all means promote posts from your own blog on to the SocMed, but there are some that really do need to be anchored firmly to your blog.

When your blog post is of direct, longer-term interest to your target market. This needs to stay on your own site because after the initial, rather flirtatious *frisson* on the SocMed in terms of the post's promotion, your readers want to come back to your blog so they can remain informed and remind themselves of important issues.

When your blog post is educational about something that's around for more than 5 minutes. You may - rightly - choose to comment fleetingly on the latest whizz bang toy in your industry in a blog post on LinkedIn or Google Plus, but the down-to-earth facts about the issue ... and your considered opinion ... belong on *your* site. That's where customers and prospects can be comfortable in knowing the information is there and available to them.

When your post is about something that may lead to a sale. Never forget that we're all in business to make a living. Particularly if your blog post is connected with or part of your main commercial website, anything relevant that you write should be published on and be promoted towards *your site* ... not the general airwaves of SocMed.

Key point to remember about blogging away from your own site

Well, I think it's a key point, anyway! As I mentioned in the introduction, your "owned content" is becoming increasingly important now that the social media platforms, having worn out their enthusiasm for philanthropy, are eager to monetize their businesses.

As your blog is a very important part of your owned content, in your shoes I would never be tempted to put blogging on a social media platform before doing so on my own site.

By all means use the social media platforms to share your ancillary news and views, but always make sure everything you do is anchored, somehow, to your "owned content," and that whatever you publish goes on your own blog first before it appears anywhere else.

At the time of writing the jury is still out on how Google will consider your articles posted on social media platforms. But one thing is for certain – if you publish on your own site first, that's where you'll get the Google brownie points. And that's where you want them.

WRITING STYLE TIPS

Do you believe that anyone can write a blog post? It's true, but many people fall down on the style and tone of their text. Often, you'll find people write as they think they should come across, rather than as who they really are.

That is forgivable if you're writing a formal business proposal or a keynote speech for a conference, but in blogging it's a real no-no.

Blogging is all about being yourself, being informal and sharing a conversation with your readers that they can understand and identify with.

Write for your audience as yourself-the-human-being

A very interesting issue often comes up in workshops I give for senior professionals who need to write text for the general public.

These writing workshop participants are experts in their field and they find it hard to "detune" their vocabulary and way of communicating to the level required so that their audience can understand what they're talking about.

And when they do, they feel as guilty as hell about it, because they think they're being patronizing. They forget that simple language – as opposed to technical jargon and complex terminology – is what everyone speaks every day ... including them.

Remember what it's like to be human?

Something I have been banging on about for years is that the last person who should ever write text, a speech or anything else is an expert. Experts know too much and assume too much prior knowledge of the subject matter on the part of the audience.

However many people who come on my workshops – often experts from specialized groups in both commercial and public sectors – have to write blogs and other content for a non-technical readership whether they like it or not. They find it difficult.

Yet it's not hard for them – and others like them – to leap over the credibility barrier and communicate with their audiences in ways that work, as long as:

1. They realize they need to stop thinking (and hiding behind) "me-speak" because their readers may not understand it

2. They realize that it's OK to detune their "me-speak" – no-one is going to judge them as being inept just because they stop using long technical words

You have to get naked

That's right: strip off your uniform, your business suit, and your professional persona. Readers of blog posts – especially B2C (business to consumer) blog posts - are intimidated by all that and if you so much as utter a term they don't understand they will click right away from your text.

Especially if you're someone who is a senior expert in your field, get off your high horse and think – and write – in the sort of fashion your key audience uses. I know it's hard ... I have spent many, many hours over the last umpty-dump years re-wording information produced by "experts" in a way that mere mortals can understand.

I shouldn't say this because I might be doing myself out of some business, but hey – why not just detune your text yourself?

It's not that hard – just talk to your ordinary self

This idea of detuning your text actually shouldn't be that difficult, provided that a) you accept that you need to do it and b) you can relax and become a member of your target audience while you're writing.

When I set exercises for my blog writing workshops I ask participants to imagine they're sitting around a table with a cup of tea or coffee, explaining the topic in hand to someone like this (depending on the nature of your blog's key readers):

- A colleague, on a break or after work
- A customer during an informal meeting
- A close friend
- A bright 12-year-old
- Someone you've just met
- Someone who doesn't speak English very well
- An elderly aunt or uncle
- Etc.

Then I get them to write down what they would say in those circumstances.

If you can't write it, speak it

Quite often, workshop participants start off very well in their written attempts but sentence by sentence they creep back into their own jargon and tone of voice.

The answer here, is to forget writing for the moment, and speak the topic through. Use your phone or other audio recording device. Record it, transcribe it, and use that as the basis for your writing.

You might even find you can use voice recognition software as long as your particular program is well used to your voice and you don't have to fiddle with it while you're talking, as this will distract you.

It's very simple, really. To write effective information for the "general public," you have to strip off and become a member of the general public again, yourself. Here is some further advice which should help you avoid the pitfalls and write good, relevant, inviting text.

30 Key style guidelines for when you write a blog post

1. Before you start to write, be sure you know your readers / customers / prospects very, very well.

2. Define what you want your blog post to achieve: inform, entertain, warn, amuse, etc. Start with a short first paragraph that "hooks" the reader – remember that when you share your blog posts in the social media, often this first paragraph – or part of it – will be shown, so needs to work hard

3. Develop the basic message of that blog post out of the right criteria (what do they need and want to read, not just what you want to tell them). Use a catchy headline that offers some implied or actual benefit to the reader

4. Write as people speak: imagine you're talking to a friend over a cup of coffee, and write it down in that way

5. Write in terms of "we" and "us" or "I" and "me," but don't use a pompous "royal we" approach

6. Make every sentence relevant to the audience - "what's in it for them?"

7. Wherever possible write to "you" - not to 3rd-person "customers," "staff," "suppliers," etc

8. Don't just get to the point - start with it, and phrase it so it will grab the audience's attention

9. Say what you mean and don't procrastinate with fuzzy language

10. Be informal but be careful not to be overly familiar

11. Use action words, not passive - sharper nouns, stronger, shorter verbs

12. Use active rather than passive phrasing ("go to bed now," not "it's time you went to bed")

13. Although simple is usually better, don't over-simplify - it can seem childish or patronising

14. Don't go into more than one idea per sentence

15. Write so that one sentence flows logically into the next

16. One-word or verbless sentences are useful for pacing and effect, but only if you use them sparingly

17. Where possible start new paragraphs with links like "Of course," or "However," to keep the audience hooked

18. Use a list or bullet points to put across more than two or three items in a sequence

19. Keep jargon to a minimum and be sure your audience will understand what you do use

20. Avoid meaningless or valueless clichés because they make your writing seem unoriginal

21. Learn the difference between poor clichés and your business's commonly used terms, and use the latter intelligently

22. Avoid adjectives and superlatives that smell phony, e.g. "best," "fastest," "exciting"

23. Use the most visual adjectives and adverbs you can think of - they're powerful

24. Use "Plain English" wherever possible and especially when writing for audiences whose mother-tongue is not English

25. Avoid long blocks of text because they're uninviting to read, especially online

26. Visually break up continuous sections of text by peppering them with cross-headings or emboldened key points –this way readers can scan the post to get the essential points and go back to read it in full later. Useful for readers in a hurry!

27. Keep paragraphs short, and vary the length of sentences from short to medium-length. People's views vary a lot about how long a text blog post should be. Some say keep it short (200-300 words) whereas others say you can go on up to about 1,500 words. Given that readers don't want to feel cheated at seeing a very short piece – but don't have time to read a very long one – I reckon a safe guide is 500-1,000 words.

28. Check for small grammatical and punctuation goofs – they make you look amateurish

29. Check for spelling mistakes and don't rely totally on your spellchecker

30. Proofread your work backwards – it sounds crazy but you don't miss spelling or other mistakes that way

THE A–TO–Z SECTION

I've arranged the following sections in alphabetical order so you can dip in and out of what you want and need to know right now, rather than have to search for it in longer chapters. Hope this system works well for you.

ADVERTISING

Many people still think their blogs are a good place to advertise their products and services. They are wrong. Why? Because blogs are about connecting with customers and prospects on a personal basis which is linked to your business relationship – not hard sell.

OK - this can be the background build-up that supports sales, but to shove sales stuff down readers' throats here is about as appropriate as hard-selling ice cream to people whose freezers have just broken down.

It's all about relationships, hence blogging

I know, I know. Everywhere you look on the internet and particularly within Social Media we're talking about developing and nurturing relationships before anyone tries to sell something to someone. And in all honesty, that's probably right.

For too long we have been pestered by high-powered selling through the media whatever the media chosen to make it happen, and people are – frankly – fed up with it. Even though I'm a marketing-based business writer by trade, I feel disgruntled when I scroll through my junk file deleting endless emails of bullsh*t purporting to be of genuine interest to me.

How can we promote our businesses by nurturing relationships via blogs?

1. **By being yourself.** One of the most wonderful things the internet and its derivatives have done for us is to freeze off a lot of the old advertising hot air that was being spread around on terrestrial media and instead focus both advertisers and customers/clients on what really matters. It's a joy to see how business honesty is appreciated by customers and clients now, whether they want to buy low-priced cosmetics or multi-thousand business systems.

2. **By leaping over a lot of corporate crap, even if you're a corporate blogger.** Blogs are personal vehicles of communication and should anyone misuse this medium and try to sneak in a par-boiled corporate message, readers will get that hint right away ... and move on. No matter how sneakily a corporate psychologist might try to wangle a sales message into a robust company blog post, readers (and customers) will figure it out. People are like that.

So should we assume a business blog can't sell at all?

No. Of course it can sell, but the sales element has to be built up on mutual trust and confidence with readers/customers. This can take time, and rightly so. Would you automatically buy a product or service from a blog that you've only just signed up for?

OK, maybe you would if the offer is good enough. But in the main, you'd need time to figure out if this product or service really is for you.

BLOG POSTS AS A BOOK

If your nonfiction/business blog posts form a coherent series – or, as we do on HTWB quite a bit – you actually write specific series of posts about a topic within the greater remit of your blog, from start to finish – you could well be sitting on the potential for a very good, well structured and successful nonfiction book.

Not long ago fiction author and expert Lucy McCarraher launched her new book, "**How To Write Fiction Without The Fuss**" which is a compilation of the superb series of tutorial articles she wrote for us on HTWB. Not only is the book a brilliant, uncomplicated way for you to learn how to write good fiction that sells … also, the book's structure works superbly. Why?

Obviously, Lucy's expertise is the number 1 reason. But beyond that, it's because the book is based on the way a series of "how to" blog posts needs to work … combining onwards flow with standalone credibility for each "episode," so allowing people to pick up the topic, read a short segment, put it down again and then go back to it later without having to run through a lot of earlier material to catch up on what has gone before.

So, how should you organize your blogs if there's a potential book in them?

Needless to say a lot depends on the nature of your blog.

If it's about one very specialized niche topic...

... consider organizing your posts so that they flow from one end of a process to another.

For example, if you write about garden design, you could put up a series of posts on how to design a new garden from scratch. Let's say your readers either have moved into a brand new house with nothing but some turf/sod grass in the back garden/yard, or have otherwise inherited a pile of weeds and junk.

You could then take them on a journey from there, through all the stages they need to work through right up to and including planting, nurturing and ultimate enjoying a beautiful new garden. You might want to tighten up the niche further by focusing purely on new-build property gardens that are small, and for families on a low budget.

Hence, a series of blog posts for your readers to follow and a book at the end of it called "How To Create A Gorgeous Garden On A Budget - From Scratch." (And from a marketing point of view, you could contact the developers/real estate brokers selling brand new homes and suggest maybe they use your book/eBook as a promotional piece...at a price!)

If your blogsite is like HTWB and covers a variety of related topics

... in some ways it's easier to isolate a specific series and develop those into a book. As you've seen, Lucy McCarraher's series on fiction writing became "How To Write Fiction Without The Fuss." And in a reversal, Lynn Tulip's excellent series "The Write Way To Get A Job" was based on her very successful book, "Get That Job" (So bear in mind this process can work two ways.)

So how can you look to the future book potential within your own blog?

As you'll have gathered already, think in terms of series, not one-offs.

Needless to say I do lots of one-offs on HTWB and that's fine, especially if you're posting nearly every day as I do and cover a wide variety of topics and issues.

But if you blog on a smaller scale, think how you can share your expertise and interests in a linear way (as opposed to a random way) in your blog posts, so that one day they may well fall into a cohesive structure that forms the basis of a very successful book.

And don't worry that your audience might not want to buy your book because they could view each instalment on your blogsite for free, although in theory that's true. Readers don't have time to scroll through, bookmark, download and print out endless stuff from your site: they will pay for the convenience of a contained product.

This is particularly relevant if it is a) offered as a print book as well as an eBook/Kindle and b) is the sort of book people will want share with friends and family as a gift for birthdays, Christmas, etc.

It's also very relevant if it contains information that will help people in business or whatever enterprise your topic involves; people buy business / self-help / developmental books in their droves. Do some research and you'll see where your book-based-on-your-blog will fit in.

Is it a blog, is it a book, or is it a blook?

Sometimes an idea for a book might work better as a blog – which eventually can become a book (or more) as well. The two can work symbiotically for a classic win-win exercise ... here's how.

I was working with a group of writers the other day and one of them was discussing his ideas for a nonfiction memoir (book.) After a short time it became obvious that his concept was not just one book, but potentially three or four.

To try to shoehorn that many angles into one book would have created a rather messy mishmash, and both my fellow author-tutor and I agreed that it wouldn't work.

The poor guy looked a bit disappointed until I told him that his material would be perfect for a blog.

Being an older man he wasn't familiar with how that could work, but once we had explained it he went away with the URL for WordPress and a gleam in his eyes.

This is nothing new, of course. I'm sure you've heard of a number of books that started out as blogs. In fact in the USA they now have an annual awards process for blogs that became books called "**The Blooker Prize,**" with "**blooks**" being the ensuing hybrid.

One such "blook" even went on to become a "flook" starring Meryl Streep and Amy Adams – a movie of the journal called "**Julie and Julia**" by Julie Powell, the true story of how and why she made every single recipe in the late Julia Childs' cook book.

However it's not always a matter of lifting a selection of blog posts straight into book format. Editing obviously is needed, and you may want to adjust content, too, once you have seen how it works in your blog.

Although Julie Powell's "blook" was mainly singular and linear in nature, where I think the blog-rather-than-book-to-begin-with approach is especially useful, is for anyone who – like the man at the writing workshop – has more than one stream to the message they want to share. Here are some examples:

Memoir/autobiography
- Your poverty-stricken childhood in India
- Your career as an engineer in daunting circumstances
- Your success at overcoming depression

How-to book
- Organic vegetables and green growing
- The best way to plan and run an organic vegetable plot
- Recipes for delicious organic vegetarian cuisine

Modern history

- The allied armed forces' activities in northern Europe during WW2
- The effect of the Nazi occupation on the local population in northern Europe
- The "warbrides" who went to North America after WW2
- How the influence of WW2 affected the "baby boomer" generation

Blogging is particularly flexible...

As you know, a blog offers you the option not only to publish chunks of information in short, easily digestible posts, but also it lets you choose between making those posts linear or non-linear in content. You can even post consecutively about utterly different aspects of your theme, if you want to, then file them into categories which a blog supports easily.

Print books certainly can't offer that kind of versatility and even eBooks, Kindle and the others aren't anything like as flexible.

...and interactive

The other useful aspect of a blog is that it's interactive – readers can comment on your posts and your ultimate book text grows and evolves organically. You will learn much more about your target audience this way than with pretty well any other type of research.

Your blog and book, properly configured and promoted, not only complement each other, but also help sell each other.

Much as you may think people won't want to buy your material in book form if they can read it (or similar) for free online, it doesn't work that way. Once you develop your book it will reach a slightly different or at least adjacent audience, for starters, and in any case people who may only dip in and out of a blog now and again will appreciate having everything together in one print or electronic volume.

Then, of course, the fact that you have gone into more than one stream of your material on your blog, you effectively will have laid the foundations of more than one book. Whether you actually go on to create more than one book will depend on how each stream of information is received by readers; a blog is a superb market testing tool.

BLOG POST SHARING GROUPS

Many of us belong to business blog post sharing groups whereby whenever a member publishes an article (post), the other members of the group are encouraged to share it across their own contacts and platforms.

This way each member's business blog posts get promoted, with resultant exposure across social media etc., to many times more contacts than they would be able to reach promoting blog posts on their own.

In theory, this is a great idea. In fact I belong to a few of these groups and they work quite well.

But there are some key provisos that I feel we should take seriously into consideration if the concept is going to work well, especially long term.

The social-social sharing model: why it can be tricky

Much as it's great in theory to share each other's business blog posts among a group of social (in the old sense!) and/or business friends, sometimes you'll find yourself agreeing to share posts that really don't have much or any relationship with your own business and interests.

This can lead you to feel guilty about sharing posts that have nothing whatsoever to do with your business, even on your social-social SocMed pages, because they just don't fit with what you do or who you are.

What if you don't like the other business blog posters' material?

You see this happen particularly in groups and communities set up as very well meaning and productive blogging competitions or challenges.

Despite the extremely honourable reasons why such groups and communities are set up, some of the blog posts that will be included by challenges a) won't have anything to do with what you do, and b) may not be of the sort of standard you like to keep in your own blog posts and shares.

What do you do? Go along with the rules and share the posts you're not comfortable with? Or not share, and risk being seen as not participating fully?

Commercially-based business blog post sharing groups

I've bumped into a few of these groups recently and although I certainly can see the logic and wisdom behind that thinking, my feeling is that the way it all works out in practice is not as beneficial as it may seem at first.

To begin with, the groups concerned have a somewhat too loose association across their members. OK, the members may all be small businesses, or local businesses, but if - as a group organizer - you're going to make a group like this pay, you'll probably need to be open to taking on quite a wide variety of business types. And those business types may not want to share the posts of others which either don't complement their own social media marketing activities, or don't fit in with their own particular standards.

Once again, what do the group members do? Although of course they are offered a range of other services for their money including weekly reminders, editing, SEO, etc., should they be expected to share blog posts that are totally unrelated to their own businesses - or risk being asked to leave the group concerned?

Where such business blog post sharing can work

Much as it may be tempting to create a business blog post sharing group that's based on locality or (generic) business type - e.g. (NAME OF CITY) solopreneurs / SMEs /networkers etc - I would be much more attracted to joining a group that's based on industry type.

OK, you might want to instigate a rule that says there can only be one of any type of specialist practitioner in the group - much along the lines of many F-2-F "lock-out" networking groups - to reduce the risk of competitive elements.

But within that, **a group that allows you to share posts from experts who genuinely are allied to your own area of expertise, makes a whole lot of sense.**

After all, many of us do this anyway, in an informal and ad hoc way. To formalize it shouldn't be that difficult and with the addition of ancillary services, could be a useful business model.

BULLSH*T

Although business blogs are entitled to be opinion pieces rather than straight, hard reportage, when it comes down to the crunch, your opinion by itself – no matter how much of an expert you are - usually isn't enough.

After all, despite the informality and intimacy of the blog culture, if you want to be credible in a business context to your readers, you want to make sure that what you write isn't hot air, yes? And unless you are a very well recognised expert in your field, this needs to be backed up - or it could be seen as bullsh*t.

And come on … don't you agree that there are far, far too many business blog posts floating around in the cyber-wilderness which are utter, unmitigated bullsh*t? If you don't know what I'm talking about, just check your junk mail folder. So you can't blame readers (and your potential customers) for being a little sceptical about what you say, unless you can back it up powerfully.

The answer?

Combine these two magic ingredients

One: fact-checked information. This is your key bullsh*t deterrent. Don't assume, and don't paraphrase unless you know the topic very,

very well. It may take a little time but hey – in the current climate your business blog is becoming increasingly valuable as a pivotal marketing tool for your entire business. So it's worth spending time on it. And soon you'll get used to searching for facts and figures on Google with clarity and accuracy.

Two: your opinion, slant, take, view, whatever you call it, based on this fact-checked information. This is not an ego trip or bragging: it's what makes your blog post unique, even though hundreds or even thousands of other people may have written about the same topic. And it's what your customers / clients, prospects and other readers will value because it's unique to you, whom they like and trust. Don't undervalue your opinions on business topics related to your own business: you matter, and what you think and say matter, too. Be bold, on the strength of accurate information and informed, clear vision.

Why so many bullsh*t business blog posts still hang around

Once again, take a look in your junk folder. Personally I think some of these bullsh*tty sites keep going because they somehow have slipped under the radar of Google's more recent algorithms designed to rid the blogosphere of such muck.

However business blogging bullsh*t is likely to continue lurking, perhaps under more sophisticated guises, but nonetheless far into the future.

Don't let your business blog fall into that unpleasant and unprofitable trap.

CASE HISTORIES AS BLOG TOPICS

Case histories are a very good source of inspiring blog posts. Written up as a single or series of posts, they're OK provided that they're not boring, and clearly demonstrate a learning point about topics that are relevant to readers.

Studying case histories (not necessarily written as posts) will tell you a lot about your customer base and the issues they face, which should supply you with further ideas for posts.

For your blog you obviously need to keep the case histories fairly short, because in an ideal world your blog posts shouldn't go much over 1,000 words in total and in fact can be quite a bit shorter than that.

Why case histories?

Nearly everyone enjoys a good story, and case histories – or at least the worthwhile variety – are just that. If you are in close contact with your customers or clients you'll know what they're up to and how your work is helping them. But as this is a blog, not a press release or other promotional piece of writing, you don't want to use the case history as a way of blowing your own trumpet.

A better way of approaching it is to ask your clients or customers to share their own journeys through business and offer advice to your readers, tips on what to avoid, what works, what doesn't. This opens the case history out, and makes it much more interesting, to a wider audience.

And although your part in the customer's overall story may be small – e.g. you supply them with office stationery or software support, the fact that the story is on your blog in the first place is a sufficient endorsement for you.

Don't forget that although you may only supply their office stationery or software support, the prospective customers you're aiming for are likely to have businesses not unlike the one in the case history. So they're bound to be interested in hearing how someone else copes with all sorts of business challenges – not just the ones you solve with your products or service.

Getting hold of case histories

Rather than just chart the overall story of a customer or client (although in the absence of a topical issue that can work), it's worth trying to hang the case history on a particularly interesting topical event or activity of theirs.

So, keep track of your customers or clients and what's happening to their businesses. Watch out for any mention of them in local or other media. Did they just …

- Win an award?
- Just get a big new contract?
- Start recruiting for several new jobs?
- Raise money for charity?
- Open a new factory?
- Win a big export order?
- Sponsor a charity fundraiser?

Include some good quotes

I have written about this before about case histories but please remember a) to include some short, sharp quotes from key people in the story and b) get the quotes to be part of the story, not the awful old "corporate speak" garbage you so often see.

Interview your clients over the phone, in person or via email, and extract quotes that actually form part of the narrative, not corporate wind. For more about getting good text-based interviews, go to the interviews section.

CHILDREN AND FAMILIES AS BLOG TOPICS

You'd be surprised how many links there are from businesses to children and families generally, even when the product or service concerned isn't obviously connected with those topics. However, let's start by looking at businesses that do have a connection.

Business connected with children and families

Here are a few trigger points you might like to think about for blog posts that are not necessarily related to your product or service, but which will be of interest to parents and other family members who are your current and prospective customers...

- Practical safety for children – in the home, outdoors, while walking, cycling to school, in cars, etc.
- Safety from strangers
- How to choose the right schools
- Bullying at school and among peer groups
- School problems and how to solve them
- ADHD and other behavioural problems
- Autism Spectrum, Aspergers, etc
- Family holidays, vacations
- What to do in the school holidays

- Child-friendly food and recipes
- Fun things to do on a rainy day
- Nurseries, pre-school, day care
- Elderly relatives – care homes, nursing homes, independence
- Family arguments and tensions
- Step families
- Family occasions, e.g. religious events, birthdays, etc – organizing, planning, shopping for, etc.
- …and so-on.

What if your business is not directly child/family related?

OK, let's take some examples of businesses in this category and see what child/family related topics could bounce off them…

Plumbing business – toilet training for toddlers, bathroom hygiene, conserving water, safety of drinking tap water, health hazards in the shower, making bath times fun, safety in the bathroom for seniors

Business coaching – life-work balance, how to cope when your child wants you to stay home for the day, keeping family out of your home office, explaining modern tech to elderly relatives, dealing with partners' professional jealousy, how to cope with your business during pregnancy

Web design business – design and accessibility of websites for kids / seniors / people with disabilities, review of best children's websites, showing seniors how to use the web and surf, most child-friendly and most senior-friendly phones, tablets, laptops, etc, parental internet controls, reviews of latest children's games

Construction equipment/plant hire company – safety when there are children and/or seniors around, what to consider when using equipment near schools, care homes, playgrounds, etc, review of best toy tractors, bulldozers, backhoe loaders, etc, why little boys love to play with toy excavators etc, interviews with senior former users talking about their memories of this equipment when they were young, pictures and description of machines back through history.

But all these topics are covered in magazines

Yes, they are. But they're covered by other people, and people who don't know anything about your business and your customers.

What makes the blog posts you write on these topics unique is because they are your take on them, and the way you relate the information to your own very specific audience. That makes them well-targeted and much more interesting to your readers than the generalized stuff they can pick up on the internet or in the papers.

So off you go – use your imagination with the help of your inner child!

COMMENTS

When you read an article or blog post online and at the end it says something like, "have your say: put it in here..." do you really feel inspired to jump into the conversation? Or do you think, from the invitation you've seen, that the writer/blogger really couldn't care less what you think but wants some extra traffic from whatever bullsh*t you might write in a comment?

Good "posticles" and "artiposts" attract comments

...and of course they deserve to. I love the comments I get on HTWB and always respond to them, because – frankly – if nothing else, it's only polite. If someone takes the trouble to share an opinion on a "posticle" of mine it's only good manners for me to answer that comment.

Often the comments and discussions take place elsewhere – say, on LinkedIn, Facebook or Google Plus – and equally I acknowledge and respond to these, too. That's all part of the current spread of blog commenting across the social media.

Wherever the comment is located, in 99 percent of cases the point the commenter has made is very valid, adds an extra dimension to the discussion, and turns my necessarily one-dimensional OP into a conversation that is useful and beneficial to all who take part.

HOW TO WRITE BRILLIANT BUSINESS BLOGS

Some bloggers just don't give a sh*t

What really makes me angry is the way in which some bloggers and other online communicators devalue people's views purely by intimating, in their blog posts, articles, web content and more, just how little respect they have for what others have to say.

Typically it can be interpreted as "oh, by the way - we've put a little box down underneath this text and we want you to write whatever junk you like as long as it's not spam, so Google sees that we've got lots of comments."

Talking of spam...

Some bloggers, especially, break out into a pustulating rash at the mere sound of the S word and issue vicious warnings to any commenters with the audacity even to suggest they are not there purely as philanthropic angels who have no desire to earn a living, only contribute great wisdom for the greater good.

OK, we all get the spam comments coming into our sites, and some of them are so awful they're hilariously funny.

But as for writing sheer vitriol all over your site that spammers will not only be deleted but also hung, drawn, quartered and fed to your ravening Rottweilers – get a life, for Heaven's sake. There are lots of easy plug-ins you can use to filter out spam and save your reputation and your blood pressure.

69 | P a g e

And if all else fails? Pssssttt....somewhere on your keyboard is a little button with the word "delete" written on it. Use it.

WordPress: are you listening up?

Much as I love my dear, sweet WordPress site, I really would like to see more imaginative "comments" options that don't make people who want to get involved in a discussion here feel that all their valuable opinion is worth is just as a "comment."

Or even, Heaven forbid, as it currently appears as a default on many WordPress sites - "Speak Your Mind?"

Why the hell should I "speak my mind" when you phrase your request as if you're expecting an indignant rant from an 85-year-old complaining about dog poop on the street at a local Church council meeting?

If I bother to add something to your online discussion it's not just me "speaking my mind" to a mute computer screen: it's me giving up my valuable time and brainpower to a) take you and your text seriously which it possibly doesn't deserve and b) attempt to make some sense out of it, or even praise it if it isn't utter crap.

OK, so what's the solution?

As I am saying that terms like "comments," "speak your mind," etc., are inadequate and the views of readers of blog posts and other online articles should have a higher status, my next question is... how do we do that?

This is an issue that not only WordPress, but many other platforms might like to consider.

Here are just a few of the words which, if used to replace "comments" would at least show more respect for what readers have to share. Taking that a stage further, each of those words could be prefixed with something like *"please share your (word/words) here,"* rather than the dreaded *"speak your mind."*

1. Assessment
2. Conclusions
3. Impressions
4. Observations
5. Opinion
6. Perspective
7. Point of view
8. Take on it
9. Thoughts
10. Viewpoint

Currently on HTWB, the keyword is "thoughts," which most people like. Be sure a similarly acceptable word is used on your blog. Please.

COMMENTS, MODERATING

What do you do if you get a comment on your blog that says you're wrong? Calls you an idiot? Trashes your reasoning?

Dump it into the trash box, of course. But … wait a minute…

Negative comments can be quite useful

OK, if the comment turns out to be a flame-throwing rant from someone who's in need of a personality transplant, there really isn't much you can do other than trash it.

But some negative comments can give you the opportunity to turn the criticism around through reasoned argument and show the commenter – and your readers - how, and why, the commenter's assumptions were erroneous.

I have to admit I don't often get negative comments but when I do, I don't trash them unless they're abusive or stupid, because I like to use them to make a point in the way I have just described.

Nobody is obliged to think you're perfect and everyone is entitled to disagree with you as long as they're doing it for the right reasons. **If nothing else, a comment that disagrees with what you have posted is a good starting point for a lively discussion among you and your readers.** There's nothing like a bit of dissent (as long as it doesn't get nasty or rude) to spark off people's ideas and creativity.

So if you do get a negative comment, don't be in any hurry to delete it. And when you respond, be polite and respectful. Your blog is not the place for a slanging match.

Spammy comments

If you're using a WordPress or Blogger site, or another that's well structured, you'll have a spam Rottweiler built into the site that will gonzo all obvious spam, so you don't need to worry about it.

But sometimes you get borderline posts that may contain a link to something else, but nonetheless add value to the conversation you've started.

Tip: don't be annoyed that someone has posted a comment with an external link in it. This does not necessarily mean your readers will be sidetracked to some seedy site selling Viagra clones and porn videos.

Check the link out, by all means. And if it's a relevant article or blog post, comment on that yourself with a link back to your own site.

After all, that's what social media is about – conversations, and conversations across more than one platform.

Nice-but-bland comments

Never ignore them. Respect the fact that someone has taken the trouble to comment on your post, even if it is just to say "hey, I enjoyed this" (unless they come from a URL that's selling Viagra.)

Depending on which blog system you use, you'll soon learn how to tell the genuine comments from the phony, spammy ones that manage to get through your filters – and some still do.

With genuine commenters, the very least you can do is to thank them for calling by your site and ask them to keep in touch.

Use commenters' names when responding

This differentiates your response from a somewhat robotic-sounding "thank you for commenting," which doesn't fool anyone: it's a way to generate more Google-smacking noise.

It also tells the original commenter that it's you, not some machine that read their comment and responded to it. You'd be surprised how such small courtesies can help build and sustain relationships with people who, if not already, may well become your customers/clients one day.

Don't be afraid of going off-topic

If the conversation veers off into related but different areas, don't worry about it. It's all good stuff and helps to cement relationships with your commenters.

You can always nudge the conversation back towards the main topic a bit later on, if you want to.

How to bring conversations back to your blog

This may seem a bit maverick-like, but if a discussion about a post I have promoted on a social media platform takes place in a public group or forum (so is in the public domain) if it's interesting enough I cut and paste the whole thing and insert it as a comment back on the post concerned on HTWB.

If the conversation has happened in a closed or private group and I feel others would benefit from sharing what was discussed, I ask the other commenters for their permission and once I receive it, again – I cut and paste the discussion into a comment space on HTWB.

As of 2014 Google Plus has a plug-in for WordPress that automatically transfers all conversation about a particular post that happens on G+, back as comments on your own blog. Once it's there, you can then add more comments and responses and insert "plus ones" and those not only are included on your site, but also are transmitted back to Google Plus. I really hope the other main business social media platforms follow their example.

COMMENTS, YOURS ON OTHER PEOPLE'S BLOGS

When you comment on a blog post written by someone else, contrary to some people's opinions it actually does get noticed ... by other readers, of course, and also by Google et al. And it all helps to keep those conversations moving in the right directions.

But what do you say? Here are my own 10 tips on how to avoid writing bad comments that die a death for you, your business, your reputation and more....

1. **Don't go "off topic."** Not only is this distracting to readers of the whole blog, but also it's incredibly rude to the original poster.

2. **Don't be afraid to disagree.** Disagreement is fine within comments provided that a) it's respectful and b) relevant.

3. **Don't introduce notions that aren't directly connected with the original post.** You might see a connection, but make sure you've thought through whether other readers would agree with that.

4. **Don't lose your temper, no matter how much you disagree with what the poster has said.** Blog posts with comments are not battlefields; they are, or should be, fora

(that's the plural of forum, OK?) for eloquent and informed debate. That means no four-letter words, flames, or bitchy rants...

5. **Don't add anything to the thread that's anything other than useful and interesting.** This can happen in a number of ways, but always be conscious of the original poster's point and develop your comment on that basis.

6. **Don't add an irrelevant experience of your own** ... but by all means add one which either agrees with the poster's notion, or perhaps disagrees with it (provided that you explain why you think there is an alternative way of looking at it.)

7. **Don't use a blog comment to sell your own product or service.** If, however, something you sell or do is DIRECTLY relevant to the original post, you could mention it as an option for readers to consider. But hard sell is a BIG no-no.

8. **Don't be afraid to cut and paste bits from the original post,** or – where relevant – from other topics. Readers are not clairvoyant and most will not spend time scrolling up and down to find out what bits from the original post or other comments you're referring to. Cut and paste such sections into your comment and put quotation marks (inverted commas) around them, then make your own comments directly underneath.

9. **Don't be pompous, condescending or boring.** Face it —
those of us the wrong side of 50 may have loads of
experience and all that, but we're not necessarily "up there."
Even if we are, appreciate the readership of the blog
concerned and write for it, not against it.

10. **Don't lose your sense of humour.** Blog post comments
are, of course, serious and very meaningful in the main, but
a touch of humour helps everyone assimilate the serious
content and also enjoy the experience.

CROSSHEADINGS

Using crossheads when you're composing your blog post is important for a number of reasons. Here are some of them.

First of all, what is a crosshead? *(this is one, FYI…!)*

Basically, a crosshead is a subheading or secondary headline that encapsulates in a few words what's to come in the ensuing paragraphs of text.

Although internet writing wallahs think they've invented these devices, they haven't – those of us who have been writing promotional material in the offline world have been using them for years.

Why? Because they help you plan your text, break it up, and give the small print something to hang off.

Use crossheads in your first draft to anchor your thinking

Although you may edit and/or change them for the final draft of your business blog post, writing roughly right crossheads before you write anything else will help keep you on the straight and narrow of your topic.

Essentially they pinpoint the key messages that you want to get across, and focus your mind on those ... which stops your mind wandering off into tangents which may or not be relevant for this particular section of your blog post.

Use crossheads to help your post flow

Writing crossheads can be a very useful way for you to focus on the overall flow of what you want to share in your blog post.

And by writing out your crossheads before you get into more detail, you're in effect creating a skeleton of your blog post which forms a solid and relevant structure for the final draft. This is invaluable.

At this stage, too, if you feel your text might not be moving in quite the right direction, it's one hell of a lot easier to shift content around at the crosshead stage, than it is when you have written out your entire first draft.

So with your final choice of crossheads in place, in the right order, you can then go on to flesh out your key points in detail.

Use crossheads to capture the attention of scanners

It's well known that people reading pretty much anything online now are very short on time and are likely to scan a blog post that interests them to get the essential gist of what it offers ... perhaps reading on if they're really interested, or if not, at least taking note of the post and who wrote it.

This is where crossheads really can gel: provided that you get the key points of your post across in the crossheads ... if relevant with a call to action in there prominently ... readers won't necessarily have to scroll back through the whole thing to get your message.

Make sure that your call to action smacks them straight in the teeth

With the right crossheads culminating in a good call to action, readers will have your story presented to them in a series of sequential bullet points that should get them right where you want them.

Crossheads are very valuable, so make use of them.

CURATION

Content curation has become a very powerful tool in the inbound marketing mix – provided you know how to do it, and use it, properly.

Because I am a relative beginner at content curation, I asked Winnipeg-based professional writer and content curator **Cendrine Marrouat** to share her tips on how to make content curation work for you…especially relevant as a tool in your armoury for business blog writing. Here she is…

Whenever someone asks me what activity has given my personal brand the biggest boost, I automatically answer "curation."

I may love sharing my thoughts and tips with my audience, but I enjoy putting other worthy creators in the limelight even more. I find it a very complementary process that allows me to continue helping my audience, while not having to constantly come up with new ideas for articles.

Every day, millions of pieces of content are indexed in search engines. Unfortunately, most of the quality stuff is often buried under a pile of bad content. So, finding what you need can be very challenging – unless you can afford to spend 6 or 7 hours scouring the Internet every day.

That is where content curation comes into play. By separating the wheat from the chaff, curators fill an important need. Not only do they provide their audiences with great answers, but they also do it in a way that saves people a lot of time.

Curation: what is it?

Digital curators collect and sort through the huge masses of content, decide what pieces they will share, and organize them into specific categories.

We are all curators in a way. After all, who does not like to share interesting information with others? However, professional curators go beyond that simple act by also adding their own voice to the mix.

Curation: benefits

Let me list a few benefits for you here. There are more, but these are a good start.

- The more interesting content you share, the more people will notice you, and the more they will want to connect with you.
- Curating value will make you a reputable source of information. It's how you build trust.
- Good curation is also about showing off your personality. In a nutshell, you are what you curate.

- As your reputation grows, people will be interested in getting to know you. A perfect branding boost!

How to find content

I have used many tools to find the content I curate. Let me share three of my favourites here:

Swayy – (http://www.swayy.co/) The service analyses your social profiles and audience's interests and then delivers the most relevant content to you. I find gems every day!

Scoop.it – (http://www.scoop.it/) Members of the site receive a daily summary in their inbox. This summary features the top stories on the topics they follow. It is a fantastic way to discover interesting content.

Curate.Me – (http://curate.me/) Curate.me finds the best stories from your Twitter and Facebook streams and delivers them straight to your inbox. I like this service, because it only sends me a couple of stories per topic.

For more tools, you can refer to the following articles on Cendrine's blog:

14 tools and services to stay on top of the news in your industry
http://socialmediaslant.com/news-monitoring-tools/

8 more tools and services to stay on top of the news in your industry
http://socialmediaslant.com/news-monitoring-tools-2/

Some tips to help you do curation the right way

Being a good curator is not rocket science. However, it requires some practice.

First, make sure you know the difference between sharing and actual curation. Telling your friends to check out an article is one thing. It is quite another to cherry pick content based on your knowledge of your audience, and then present it in a way that makes sense to them.

Another important thing is to pay attention to the way each platform you will use actually works. They all serve a different purpose!

Whenever you decide to curate something, ask yourself the following questions:

- Do I understand what I have just read / seen / listened to?
- Who is the author? Are they on Twitter, Facebook, or Google+? – Always give credit where credit is due and leave a comment on their blog too.
- How do I introduce the content to encourage my audience to read it?
- Does the title need some reworking?
- Where will I share the content?

- How will I introduce it so that it is relevant to my audience on each platform?

Answering these questions has helped me focus more on my audience and less on myself. This process has made me a better writer and professional.

The exposure I have received thanks to content curation is mind blowing! For example, I have more than 11,000 followers on Scoop.it. The competition in my industry is fierce, so these people would probably have never found me otherwise.

Conclusion: why you should curate content on your blog

When I talk to people about curation, they automatically think of sites like Scoop.it, Paper.li, or Google+. Only a few will mention their own blog.

While these platforms will certainly be beneficial, I also recommend that you take advantage of your online real estate. Here are several reasons why you should do so:

- Increasing targeted traffic to your hub.
- Cementing your relationship with followers.
- Allowing the creators you highlight to see you in action.
- Attracting influencers in your niche for potential partnerships.

At the end of the day, good blogging is about customer service. So, if you can add curation to the mix, you should start seeing more and more people flock to you for answers.

Cendrine Marrouat is a social media coach, blogger, curator, and journalist living in Winnipeg, Canada. A social media instructor, her latest blog is Social Media Slant, which focuses on social media tips, tools, stats, and news for small businesses and solo-entrepreneurs.

Cendrine is also the author of two social media books: "The Little Big eBook on Social Media Audiences: Build Yours, Keep It, and Win" (2014) and "The Little Big eBook on Blogging: 40 Traffic Generation Tips" (2012).

You can see more about Cendrine at http://www.socialmediaslant.com

Thank you, Cendrine!

CUSTOMER EXPERIENCE

Recently I heard a brilliant talk about the realities of the customer experience. I learned a lot from what the speaker shared and realized how important it is to apply her wise advice to the content of business blog posts. So here are a few things that I interpreted from her talk.

Customers don't buy products, services, or even brands: they buy experiences

Although you might think this concept is only applicable to the big consumer brands, it isn't. It goes far beyond that, right into B2B communications and right down to micro-businesses where there is just you, your coffee percolator, your dog and of course, your customer.

Everyone from Apple and Virgin downwards is now working on the customer experience and focuses tightly on how people feel about dealing with their companies, products and services. And it's not just in terms of factual stuff like product quality, technical expertise, good customer service, etc.

"We aren't in the coffee business, serving people. We're in the people business, serving coffee."
Howard Schultz, CEO of Starbucks

Of course the factual elements are important, too. But what drives the whole thing is not matter-of-fact issues: it's all about emotions - how your dealings with them make you feel.

Enter the business blog: probably the most useful tool in the box

I know I always harp on about the need for you to be yourself when you blog for business. But given what this speaker's experience and knowledge demonstrated, I could see that you need every opportunity you can lay your hands on to develop an open, honest, personal relationship with your customers.

> *"This is it - this is what matters - the experience of a product - how it makes someone feel. Stop trying to figure out how to sell something to somebody: figure out how you want your customers to feel."*
> *Ron John, Apple Senior VP*

And needless to say your business blog is the ideal medium in which to help nurture a good personal relationship with all your readers, customers and prospects. Why?

1. **Blogs are known to be the relaxed, non-pushy element of any business website.** Savvy business bloggers never take the p*ss in their posts by writing barely-camouflaged ad copy. They respect the fact that the blog area is non-salesy-pushy and just focuses on sharing information, comments,

even light-hearted content that readers will find helpful and relevant.

2. **For reasons given in #1 above, readers and customers tend to trust your blog posts** as being far less commercial than the more marketing-orientated sections of your website. So what you say in your blog posts is likely to be taken in more informally – and more personally.

3. Following on from the above, **you can use your blog to relax and kick your shoes off, metaphorically, and communicate with your readers/customers as you, the person** – rather than you, the company / brand. Much as this (initially!) may make you feel like you're walking naked in front of an audience of thousands ... once you get used to the idea of communicating with your readers/customers on this level you will get to love it. They will love you for being yourself – the person behind the brand – and you will love being able to share with them all the excellent values you offer, as a friend and colleague.

Here are the key points I learned from that very interesting talk:

1. Modern business succeeds because people like the way you and your product/service make them feel.

2. Your business blog is where you can show them how they can feel, more than any other part of your marketing mix.

3. Don't lose those opportunities.

DANGER ZONES AS BLOG TOPICS

Can there really be danger zones within business blog writing? Oh, yes. Here are the main ones you need to watch out for, whatever business you're in. You may read about certain elements in this chapter elsewhere in the book, but trust me: it's worth getting then firmly established in your sub-conscious.

So here's the stark, staring reality you need to focus on whenever you tackle some blog writing...

Business Blog Writing Danger Zone Number 1: using a blog post as a sales pitch. Tempting though it might be to use a blog post to sell your latest product or service, trust me – in the blogosphere which is a significant area of the Social Media universe, overt selling in a blog post is regarded as cheating and worse. Use your blog and its posts to build a rapport with your customers, rather as you might over a social lunch or drink or coffee after work. Leave the sales stuff for other media.

Business Blog Writing Danger Zone Number 2: poor grammar, spelling, punctuation, syntax. Those are things you need to get just about right. Not just because people will think you're a dimwit if you get them wrong, although there's a good chance they will. More importantly, it's because if you can't write coherently people may not understand what you're talking about and eventually may not understand what your business is about, what you can do for them, and how they can get you helping them.

Business Blog Writing Danger Zone Number 3: allowing your content to drift off into areas of no interest to your readers / customers. Especially if you're short of ideas on what to write about for your blog, this is easy to do – but will lose you readers ... and possibly customers or potential customers, too. Also beware people offering to write guest posts for your blog when they're trying to sell something within the blog post's text – best to avoid them if you're a beginner.

Business Blog Writing Danger Zone Number 4: being too self-focused. Much as you may feel your own experiences and opinions are interesting and valid – and I'm certain that they are – never forget that readers tend always to ask themselves that old "what's in it for me" question. Try if you can to turn your stories and information into text that involves readers – invites them into your words – so they become, and remain, involved to the end of your blog post.

Business Blog Writing Danger Zone Number 5: knocking your competitors. There's an old saying that "what goes around, comes around" and being rude about your competitors – even if you feel they deserve it – doesn't gain you any brownie points with your readers and customers. By all means draw comparisons between what you offer and what they offer, but if you want to post directly about your competitors' offerings, you would do better to draw upon external reviews, or get an unbiased guest poster to do it.

Business Blog Writing Danger Zone Number 6: not asking people to do something at the end of the post, i.e. a "call to action" sometimes affectionately abbreviated to "CTA." In my case all I do is ask people to call by my Bookshop on their way through and/or sign up to Blog Writing News. But if you have a particular offer or other promotion you are running, be sure to use this opportunity.

Don't forget – remind yourself of these criteria as often as possible…

EDITING

Editing is a topic writers (and editors, natch) have been arguing about for decades, if not centuries.

Writers often say that (nonfiction, especially) editors are ruthless butchers who shred good writing right down to its knickers... and impose all kinds of their own suppositions on someone else's stuff, so nixing all creativity on the author's part and turning the text into robot-speak nonsense.

Nonfiction editors often say that writers think they can bore readers with their elaborately and painfully long expositions of their own thoughts when in fact all readers want to know is the facts without the bullsh*t, especially if it is long-winded.

Both are right, but both can be wrong, too.

When it comes to business blog writing, we bloggers in 99 percent of cases do not have ruthless and unsympathetic editors breathing down our necks which is a mercy.

But ... this means we need to learn how to be our own editors, to make sure we don't write bullsh*t and/or any more text than our readers need and want to know.

Key issues about editing

Where blog posts are concerned, you need really to focus on the following points once you have written your first draft. Ask yourself the following questions:

- **Does it grab your readers by the throat in the first sentence or two? If not, it should**

- **Does it get to the point reasonably quickly, or does it waffle? If the latter, chill – a little waffle is OK amongst friends – but make sure you make some useful points pretty soon**

- **Are there any spelling, grammar, syntax or other goofs in it? Correct them. Now. These make you look unprofessional**

- **Does it conclude with a relevant "call to action?" Don't let it just dribble off – tell your readers what you'd like them to do next even if it's just to check out a website or comment on what you've just written about**

Yes, but what is editing? Really?

Is it rocket science? Or is it something anyone can learn to do, at least for their own purposes? Here's how to do it successfully...

Editing can be anything from simple correction of spelling and grammar mistakes – to a major reduction (or expansion) of the text.

However, one of the benefits of getting your thinking right before you start writing (as I always preach) is that you don't have to edit your work very much. That's because you have already done a lot of the necessary editing while thinking about your writing.

Although some people will tell you that extensive editing can only improve your work, I don't necessarily agree. Yes, it's important to make sure your text is correct and concise. But too much editing can change what you've intended completely and with that, your writing can lose its freshness and originality. That's why I feel it's better to do the structural "editing" before you write, not after.

Here, though, we take a look at how you can improve your text with some editing techniques that work after you've written the first draft.

The first point is this. If you read through your text and you feel it needs a lot of editing, think hard. Will that solve the problems? Or would it save time in the long run to discard what you have drafted and write the text again?

The same applies if you find that your text is very much too long to fit into the space required. When this happens, you can't just write the same text in a shorter way. You have to remove content, which may change the meaning and/or emphasis. If you need to shorten your text by more than about 20%, then, it is probably safer to go back to the beginning and re-write it.

Structural editing

Although you should have "edited" the structure of your text at the thinking stage, not the writing stage, you may want to check your text after you've written it to make sure it achieves your objectives.

Here are some questions to ask yourself, in this order:

1. Does it start by identifying clearly the key point of the piece – the notion?
2. Does it provide convincing and accurate information to support that?
3. Does it conclude and summarize the main issue?
4. If relevant, is there a strong call to action?

Style editing

Here is a checklist you can use after you've written your text, to make sure its style works well.

1. Take out any adjectives and adverbs that don't work hard
2. Remove repetitive words, phrases and sentences
3. Make sure each sentence flows logically into the next
4. Make sure paragraphs and sections flow in logical sequence too
5. Where appropriate use sub-headings to make text more readable and scannable
6. Run a final spell check and double check homophones, etc., yourself

Edit from screen or printed page?

Some people find that no matter how much they edit their work on a computer screen, they still find mistakes and things to improve once the text is printed out on paper.

If that's true for you, always be sure to print out your text and check it that way. I always check out my text on printed paper, but assumed it was because I am a boring old f*rt who grew up in pre-internet days.

However you might find it interesting to note that my son, who at the time of writing (2014) is 22 years old, feels exactly the same way. After 3 years as an undergraduate at university he still preferred to print out study information and read it on paper rather than on a laptop of other device.

So be kind to yourself. If you edit better on paper, print it out. Never mind the chopped-down trees.

Other people's opinions

If you're not a professional writer (and even if you are) it sometimes helps to show your text to someone else and ask their view. But be careful.

Some people will find something to criticize in your writing, no matter how small or unimportant, just because they feel it's expected of them.

If you want a balanced opinion from a colleague/friend/family member/etc., don't hand them your text and say "what do you think of this?" That invites them to be critical.

Instead, say you'd like them to imagine they're the person who will receive and read your text. Tell them the basis of your mission – what you want and/or need to achieve with this text. Then ask them how well they understand the message in that way.

Almost certainly you will get more than a "yes" or a "no." And if the person doesn't understand the message of your text in the right way, you can ask why. The answers will be less about your writing than about your thinking through of the text, which is probably where it will have gone wrong anyway.

Other people's editing

Sometimes your writing will have to be edited by others – e.g. senior colleagues – whether you like it or not.

If this happens, do not let it go to print or screen immediately. Take another look at it. The other people may be careful when editing your text. But the fact that they didn't create it to begin with means they may not have understood your objectives properly.

If someone has made a change to your text that does not work – or changes its meaning – go back to that person and discuss it with them (even if the person is your boss!) Only go ahead with the text when you and that person are both happy that the meaning is correct.

FUN

Should writing business blog posts be fun? Should turkeys avoid advertising Thanksgiving and Christmas?

To me this is a no-brainer. Why? Because blog posts need to be informal conversations with your readers. And in the majority of cases, having an informal conversation with someone about business is likely to include the occasional light-hearted moment ... a touch of humour, an amusing story.

Fun with blog posts: is this right for serious business?

OK. Maybe not if you're an undertaker.

But no matter how serious your business is otherwise - accountancy, law, pension and investment advice, and so-on - **there is always room for a bit of relaxation** in your blog posts; somewhere to keep on topic, of sorts, but also to share a bit about you and what you're like as a human being, as well as what you're like as an expert in your business field.

After all, as I keep saying: your blog is not a one-way channel for corporate or other business / marketing / sales spiel. It's a forum for developing relationships with your readers. OK, in a business context that means customers and prospects.

But hey, here's a revelation; even customers and prospects are human beings - ergo, people.

As all the contemporary marketing "experts" say, you need to build relationships with people ... get them to like you and trust you ... before they'll buy from you.

So when you write and publish the occasional "fun" blog post you'll find that can go a long way towards helping you succeed in this social process.

Can there really be relaxed fun in a corporate blog?

You may think that it's dangerous to let your guard down in your blog posts, especially if you are representing your firm, company or other corporate body.

That's one of the reasons why many blogging experts say corporate blogs should be fronted by one human being, not the entire board or a "corporate personality." Yuk.

It all comes back to the point that the main benefit of a blog for business is that it engages everyone in an informal form of communication that bypasses the "corporate voice" and gives the "human voice" a welcome chance to make itself felt.

So how do you work in some appropriate fun?

Needless to say, of course, this can and does cause major panic and stress in organizations which, prior to the advent of the internet and blogging, never have had to be more informal than smiling sweetly at each other in the restrooms of the office while sharing the hand-driers.

Here's some informal fun for you ... observed as a sign on one of those awful hot air hand driers in a corporate restroom: "Hit this button for 30 seconds of information from our company's President"

If you can't find much fun in your organization, go outside to look for it

You don't have to make jokes about your board of directors, your staff, your clients, or anyone else unless you feel that they will take it in the right way and not be offended.

However there are not many industries in which you'll find no amusing stories to be told.

Use a little imagination and some subtle Google searching and you'll discover there are interesting, entertaining stories and issues you can use in your business blog posts to add interest, colour, humour and even excitement to an area of business that most people would never have dreamed had that in its background.

What about jokes?

Hmmm ... this is a bit of a tricky area, especially (but not exclusively) if your blog writing involves an international audience.

With jokes there are a several issues to take into consideration. For more about this check out the Humour and Jokes section.

But you don't have to do jokes unless that's what you really want. Just some light-hearted, amusing and/or entertaining material will do ... to help reinforce your personal as well as professional relationships with your readers, customers, prospects and beyond.

FUTURE FOR READERS, AS BLOG TOPICS

Everyone loves to speculate about what lies ahead. However as you know, speculation comes in different shapes and sizes. Some is wild and wonderful; some is less exciting but far more realistic.

This is where you need to start using your imagination a bit and particularly, put yourself in your customers' / clients' / prospects' shoes.

To do this you don't need to be clairvoyant; you need simply to have a reasonable grasp of your industry and where it's likely to go, and where your main customers' / clients' industries' futures are concerned.

Research it, but realistically

Although if you're at the forefront of your business area you shouldn't need to look too far into the wild blue yonder, your customer / client base maybe diverse.

This means that where you need to differentiate here is between what you feel the future holds for your business, and that/those of your customers/clients.

The former is your problem. The latter is where you need to look for good blog posts. But overall you need to marry the two harmoniously.

Some examples

Your business is: garden design

Here you can pick up on the worrying thoughts of mass-produced foods, genetic modification, use of pesticides and other chemicals, etc., and encourage your readers to think organic for the future – and focus on food-producing plants that also look wonderful. Uninspired? Think "cardoons" / globe artichokes ... such imposing and stunning plants!

Composting, also, is a good one because it necessarily needs people to look to the future; using a compost container or other means takes at least a year before you get results. So does the cultivation of various perennial plants that can provide food – and beauty - for several years.

Your business is: used car sales

Depreciation of car values is often a key issue for people buying even low unit cost used cars. This can provide you with the chance to blog about the different marques and models and how their values will stand up to the test of time, and why.

As your business is used cars, you can also blog about the huge drop in value experienced in the first year when customers buy new cars, and emphasize how much better off they will be over time having bought a used car that is not subject to such galloping depreciation.

You can also look at future plans for hybrid power, hydrogen power, electrical power etc., and share your own take on all that, plus the new concept cars that festoon the motor shows but often never see the light of day. Ensure you relate all that, to your target audience which in the case of a used car business is likely to be local / regional.

Your business is: personal training

This could be really quite exciting ... what wonderful fitness products and services may be available in the future? Think how those things might affect what you do and be sure to emphasize how the human touch of personal fitness advice can never be replaced by technology.

But supervised by someone like you, the new technologies in fitness, training, etc. could offer your customers and prospects even more effective results. You could also blog about what training products and services you would like to see on the market to help your customers, and ask them to share their own views in the comments.

Your business is: running a Bed & Breakfast

Who said I don't like a challenge! LOL... Actually there is quite a lot you could blog about on this one because of the way the hospitality industry may be moving.

The fact that B&Bs are flourishing almost everywhere now suggests a turning point in people's choice of accommodation when away from home for business or recreation.

You could well blog about the fact that business people, as well as tourists, are likely to become more and more fed up with the impersonal, cloned effect of big hotels and revert to the much more intimate hospitality of the B&B.

You could also set up a survey of your readers as to why they like to stay in B&Bs rather than in cheap hotel chain accommodation, and use the results of your survey as a basis for a series of blog posts.

Key take-out point: use your imagination.

GLOSSARY FOR BUSINESS BLOGGING

Here is a very short list of key terms you'll come across when you're new to blogging. Needless to say there are hundreds if not thousands more, but these get into the realms of blog innards which when you're writing your blog posts, you don't really need to worry about much.

Article - basically, but arguably, a blog post. Some so-called experts still rant on about there being a difference between an article and a blog post, but the short answer is there isn't one. If there is a difference at all, it's that a blog post can get away with being a lot shorter than, say, a magazine article: blog posts should never really be longer than 1,000 words max, whereas a print magazine article can be twice that length. I took a very irreverent look at this issue some while back and it's still one of the most popular posts on my site, so it seems everyone is still wondering about it.

Blog – (originally "web log") Many people use the word as a noun or a verb to describe just about anything to do with blogs but let's get a bit picky here and make some sense out of it. A blog is a section of your website – or a mini-website in its own right – in which you share content (see below) including short articles known as blog posts. Lots of people try to differentiate between articles and written blog posts but nowadays essentially they're the same.

Blogging – the act of using and working on your blog ... not necessarily writing, though

Blog post – an entry that you compose and include on your blog. Can be any kind of content – text, video, audio, an infographic, etc.

Blog writing – the act of writing text to be used as a post on your blog

Blogroll - a list you see on some blogs, usually on a sidebar, giving links to other blogs the blog owner thinks are worth sharing. Not to be confused with bogroll, British English slang for toilet paper.

Blogsite – my own term for internet locations like my own, i.e. HowToWriteBetter.net, which started out as a blog but has grown to well over the size of many websites.

Blogversation – another term of mine which I have now registered as a hashtag so it's #blogversation ... the conversations that start with your blog, migrate to the social media platforms where you share news about your blog posts, and back again to your site.

Comments - what you want to people to write on your blog posts, and what you need to write on other people's blogs to share your views and your brand.

Content – the information (using all types of media) expressed on a website or blog. I hate this word because I think it's flippant and derogatory, considering all the hard work we put into creating "content," but then I'm biased...

Guest post – what it says on the label. Someone who you and your readers/customers respect sharing an article on your site. When this happens it's only a courtesy to include a short biography of the guest and include a link to his/her own site. You might also seek to guest post on others' blogsites.

HTML – Hyper Text Markup Language. This is the internet-speak version of your ordinary text, showing all the little instructions needed to make it look OK in the final version. May take you a while to understand how it works (Google it for lessons if you're keen) but in actual fact knowing its basics is very handy to make your blog posts look prettier, especially if you have a WordPress site.

Keywords – the magic word of SEO (Search Engine Optimization) and one which people drooled over in the earlier days of Google because if you got your keywords right, you got ranked high up in Google's search pages. Now not quite so important given that Google is seeing the light and focusing on what really matters, i.e. good, fresh, original and worthwhile content.

Sidebar – bit of a no-brainer when you think about it: it's the narrower column of information running down one side of a blog site's main content. Especially (but not exclusively) if you're using a WordPress site, it's very easy to add and subtract information from here and use it to promote events, activities, etc.

Widget – no, not a breed of duck, but a name for the bits and pieces you put in your site's sidebar.

Wouldn't it be nice if this list were all there is to it! But it's a start.

However there are many further terms which I suppose we should all learn. But these are the basic ones that will get us started with our business blogging.

GRAMMAR, PUNCTUATION, ETC.

I'm taking a bit of artistic licence here with grammar mistakes as I'm about to include spelling and punctuation as well, but as a whole the following goofs are almost guaranteed to make you look a bit foolish out in the business blogosphere, social media and business writing generally.

Think it doesn't matter if you make some grammar mistakes in your text?

Wrong: it does. If that offends your sense of verbal freedom, tough. Get over it, and get your writing basics right.

OK, some of your readers and customers may not mind the odd grammar mistake. But whether you like it or not, some customers will be put off by your mistakes, thinking (as many people do) that if you can't get your basic blog writing, website text and other marcom words right, what faith should they have in your business if that's the benchmark?

Need I say more?

So ignore the so-called blogging and social media experts who think it's OK to abuse the English language as in "who cares, it's only words, as long as the punters understand the message grammar and all that sh*t don't matter."

And get your head around the following classic, hugely common and so, so avoidable grammar mistakes that can make you look unprofessional and foolish.

A.M. in the morning ... needless repetition! A.M. means morning, so either say "3 a.m." or "3 o'clock in the morning." Similarly applies to P.M.

Apostrophes ... these probably cause more anxiety than any other form of writing in English, and it's utterly needless. As a general rule, you use an apostrophe 1) to show possession, e.g. "Suze's book" and 2) to create a contraction, e.g. "it's" for "it is." ("It's" and "its" can be a little confusing – see below.) You do NOT use an apostrophe for plurals of any kind – you just stick an "s" (or in some cases "es") at the end of the word. If the noun is plural, e.g. "parents," you put the apostrophe after the "s," not before, e.g. "parents' responsibility." With words like "people," "children," etc. you revert to the original format and put the apostrophe before the "s", e.g. "people's," "children's."

Brake – Break ... brake (n. and v.) is a device to stop motion, or the act of doing so ... break is to damage, often beyond repair

Capitalisation ... another one that trips up so many people, it's not funny. No matter how important you think nouns may be, there's no need to give them a capital first letter unless they are "proper" nouns – official names of people, places, organisations, countries or continents. I know that right now it's fashionable to capitalise every word in a headline or title but trust me, it's hard to read and very irritating. Do yourself a favour and capitalise only proper nouns and the key words of a headline.

Remember that just because a word seems important to you and so deserves a capital letter, it probably isn't as important to others, so just keep it all in lower case unless there are proper nouns involved.

Comprise / Consist of ... so, so many people get this wrong - especially in the real estate / estate agency business. Once and for all, here's how it works: something comprises (whatever) or consists of (whatever). Nothing ever comprises of. Ever. OK?

Definately / Definitely ... it's definitely. Definitely.

Did'nt ... Is'nt ... Would'nt ... Should'nt ... etc. WRONG! The apostrophe goes where the missing letter is, so the correct versions are didn't, isn't, wouldn't, shouldn't, etc.

Dissapointed / Disappointed ... one S, two Ps. Always.
E.G – I.E. ... not boring you with full Latin versions but e.g. means "for example" ... i.e. means "that is"

Independant / Independent ... all vowels are Es. Promise.

Irregardless ... this word doesn't exist, other than erroneously. It's either *regardless*, or *irrespective*

It's – Its ... it's is a contraction of it is ... its is a possessive pronoun like his, her, their

Lose – Loose ... lose (verb pronounced "looz") means to misplace or be deprived of something. Loose (adjective pronounced with a soft "s") means free from attachment.

Me – I ... popularly goofed when associated with another person, e.g. "Howard and me went shopping" – no! It's "Howard and I went shopping." When in doubt, remove the other person and focus on your part in it – "me went shopping?"

Prostate – Prostrate ... prostate is a gland within the male lower urinary tract ... prostrate means to lying down face down (I have even seen this mistake made in a medical PowerPoint presentation about prostate cancer. Go figure.

Rain – rein – reign ... rain is water falling out of the sky ... rein is part of horse's bridle or harness (also used as verb e.g. "to rein in) ... reign (n. and v.) = governance or office of royal person, act of doing so ... another trio of very common, classic goofs in English

There – Their – They're ... there is a place, e.g. over there ... their is something that belongs to them ... they're is a contraction of they are

Theirs – There's ... theirs means belonging to them ... there's is a contraction of there is

To – Too – Two ... to (prep.) expresses motion or direction ... too means also ... two is the number 2

Your / You're ... your means belonging to you ... you're is a contraction of you are

As you can imagine there are many, many more, but these are the main ones I see over and over again.

HEADLINES

First things first: what does the headline of your blog post have to achieve? What feeling do you want readers to have (apart from wanting to read more, obviously) once they've read it?

Fear? Curiosity? Laughter? Hope?

In both online and offline media people come up with all sorts of rationalisations about headlines needing to do this if they are in an advertisement, that if they are for a blog post, the other if they are for a magazine article, another for a press release, and so-on.

Balderdash. All headlines need to grab readers by the throat. And obviously blog posts are no exception.

Your blog post will be out there competing for attention with literally millions of others in cyberspace. Of course you can't write a headline that's going to stop the world turning on its axis. But you need to make sure yours gets noticed a) on your blog when people stop by for a look and b) in the Social Media when you and others share it.

What constitutes a good headline for a blog post?

There are thousands of experts out there in cyberspace offering you lengthy advice on this topic but in my experience here's the basic list.

A good headline has to offer something to readers that achieves one or more of the following:

1. Implies or suggests a benefit to them
2. Is genuine, relevant news they need to know
3. Intrigues them and makes them laugh
4. Needles their curiosity
5. Sympathises with their problem and hints at a solution
6. Invites them in to share what you're doing
7. Asks a question they want answered

Some popular ways of structuring good business blog post headlines

Show them how to do something ... this might be accompanied not only by text, but also by video. E.g...

*   Learn how to (solve whatever problem) in just a few hours
*   How to bypass those pesky written instructions and get your (product) working in minutes

The old list trick ... this has been around for ages but statistics show it's still a very popular pull. E.g...

*   9 ways you can beat winter blues and keep colds and flu at bay
*   15 quick tips to help you short-circuit boring office admin

Explanations of complex issues ... and how conquering those will help readers. E.g...

- Why veterinarians can gain from helping pet owners understand drug regimes
- Stop worrying about your local taxes with this easy-to-use guide

Ask a question readers will identify with... with an implied answer. E.g...

- Have you yet to discover these useful ways to cut admin costs?
- Are you still wondering why your business isn't growing as fast as you would like?

Shock, horror ... instil a little fear but make sure you ally it to salvation ASAP in the text! E.g...

- 6 warning signs that your business may be in danger of failure
- Are you sure your customers are staying loyal to you?

Goofs that could screw things up ... once again, be sure to allay fears / provide solutions ASAP in the text. E.g...

- The 6 most common mistakes naïve new SMEs make
- Are you guilty of these easily-resolved mistakes in your small business?

Sharing secrets ... I know, I know, but many people are still attracted to these headlines. E.g....

- 10 money-saving secrets that can transform your family's life
- 8 stress-busting secrets that will help you get your life back on track

And, here are some useful trigger words to start off your headlines

- Advice
- Announcing
- At Last
- Because
- How
- How To
- If
- Introducing
- New
- Now
- This
- Wanted
- Which
- Who Else
- Why
- You

Capitals in headlines and titles

I know that right now it's fashionable to capitalise every word in a headline or title but trust me, it's hard to read and very irritating. Do yourself a favour and capitalise only proper nouns and the key words of a headline, if you must, but even that can look awkward (see below).

Titles – e.g. book titles – are a little different. There are various arguments being flung around in literary circles about how to approach this one. Some purists say that every word of a title should be capitalised and that's fine if the title is short, e.g....

Business Writing Made Easy

But that becomes a nightmare (reminds me of a field full of wind turbines) when you have a longer title, e.g.

Banana Skin Words And How Not To Slip On Them

Other purists will put forward a garbled mixture of capitalised and non-capitalised words for titles based on "important" words like nouns, verbs, pronouns, adverbs and adjectives having capitals but short words like articles, conjunctions and prepositions without capitals. So you then get an even uglier mixture:

Banana Skin Words and How Not to Slip on Them
Another approach is to use all capitals for a short title:

BUSINESS WRITING MADE EASY

Which is fine, but gets a bit overwhelming with a longer title:

POWERWRITING: THE HIDDEN SKILLS YOU NEED TO TRANSFORM YOUR BUSINESS WRITING

My own view is that common sense should prevail and given that book and other document titles – and even blog post headlines - have a burning need to attract potential readers, we need to make them as visually appealing as possible and to hell with the traditional grammatically correct rules.

Use your common sense to formulate headlines that share right away what you're talking about, and make absolutely sense to your readers who will appreciate your content.

If you can, too, incorporate the appropriate keywords into that headline so Googlers find you more easily.

HEALTH AND SAFETY AS BLOG TOPICS

This may not be relevant depending on what you do, but health and safety are usually of concern if you're doing business with companies (B2B) or within consumer markets (B2C) particularly where your customers have children, animals, etc.

Health and safety for business

In the UK at least, health and safety issues have become something of a joke due to certain pieces of legislation taking on ludicrous effects in real life, and more seriously when employees hide behind H&S regulations to the extent that others can die, as was seen recently in England.

Two paramedics did a "risk assessment" where a man was drowning in a ditch and they decided it was too risky to go in and haul him out to save him, so instead they waited for back-up. A bit later a policeman arrived, quickly stripped off his outer clothes and dived in helped by two passers-by and pulled the drowning man out. However by this time the man was too far gone and was declared DOA when the paramedics finally took him to the hospital.

Check out all new legislation and set up Google Alerts (free and worth their weight in gold) for health and safety updates in your industry or business area. When an update arrives, read through the jargon and post your interpretation of how it will affect your readers/customers. They will be glad of the heads-up and also of your thoughtfulness in translating the directives into plain English.

Health and safety for families

It seems a very long time since I wrote "The Home Safety Book" but many people have since said that I should drag it out and update it as it was very popular.

If your business has any connection with the home, gardening, families, pets, medical and/or complementary treatments, etc., the occasional blog post about safety will be welcomed by your readers/customers.

To get you thinking along those lines, here is the list of chapters (copied by hand from my one remaining copy of that book!)

- Electricity
- Gas
- Water
- Fire
- Poisoning
- Do-It-Yourself work
- First Aid

- Hygiene
- Gardens and Garages
- Children
- The elderly
- The disabled
- Pets
- Crime prevention

Although you don't want to come across as a pessimistic worrier, sharing health and safety tips with both business and consumer readers/customers is certainly worth addressing once a month or so. Good luck with it!

HISTORY AS A SOURCE OF BLOG TOPICS

This may not work for every type of business but it certainly will for a great many. Not only can it be very interesting but also it can funny and entertaining. The trick is to write the historical blog posts in a light and easy-going way without boring readers with too many stuffy facts, and just picking up on the more captivating stories.

Try, too, to relate the historical content back to the present day and how the way things were back then would be seen now, especially by your customers. Don't be intimidated by what you think may be boring topics, either. There is bound to be something amusing and interesting even in the history of screws and nails...

Let's think up a few examples

OK, screws and nails!
- The first civilizations to use nails
- When someone dreamt up using a thread and making a screw
- Why threads on screws are that way around and not the other way
- Horrible accidents and crimes were committed in history, using screws and nails

Social Media

- Early storytellers
- Stories told via folk songs and poetry
- Town criers and how they worked
- Gossip and "Chinese Whispers" in centuries past
- The role of the telephone in early social media
- The lost art of letter and note writing
- Compuserve: the first live chat online?

Real estate business

- Interviews with elderly former brokers saying what it was like back in their day
- The first real estate brokers / estate agents: where it all started
- What homes sold for through the ages
- The challenges of selling homes of historical interest

Nail manicure business

- The first nail polishing in history
- What substances were used to glamorize nails through history
- Men's nails in history
- Nail fashions through the ages
- How nail polish was first formulated
- Famous nail polish manufacturers in the early 20th century
- False nails through history

Electrical engineers/contractors

- How electricity was harnessed way back when

- The very early days of using electricity for power etc.
- The first electrical engineers and how they worked
- What electricity was like when it was first introduced into homes
- What electricity was like when it was first introduced into workplaces
- The differences harnessed electricity made to civilization

Painting and decorating business
- The first interior decoration – in caves?
- Home/building decoration through the ages
- Materials used for decoration through the ages
- Dangers overcome, e.g. lead paint
- Different fashions in wallpaper through the centuries
- How interior colour preferences have varied over the last 2-3 hundred years

And so-on. Once again, a lot of this information is available in the general media, but when you write about it for your customers or clients it will be unique, because it has your stamp on it. Just be sure to know your readers well enough to judge accurately what will be of interest and/or amusement to them.

HUMAN INTEREST IN BLOG TOPICS

If you blog for business in an area that's pretty serious – law, accountancy, insurance, etc. which some might even consider as "boring" subjects – it's easy to think that you can only blog about serious business issues that some of your clients might find, well, a little on the serious, impersonal side. But that's not true.

We need to go for something better … deeper … topics that reach down further into people's hearts and minds to engage all their attention, not just the bit that deals with nuts-and-bolts business.

How on earth do these professional topics drill down into personal issues? Here's how...

Lawyers

You may think blogging for a law practice is as dry as a bone (well, a bone after it has been stripped by one of my dogs, anyway.)

So, so wrong. Why? Because although lawyers deal with dry, crisp, unchangeable law on the one hand, they deal with very human issues on the other.

At a recent networking event I spent a long time chatting with a lady lawyer who specialises in family law. She was recounting some of the vile, horrible things couples do to each other – or try to do to each other – out of spite, jealousy, anger, bitterness and numerous other awful emotions. Often at the expense of their children, too.

After I asked her whether she considered that she could often find herself in a counselling role, she admitted that she is, even though the advice she can give must, ostensibly at least, be restricted to the legal variety. But what a host of human interest blog posts her stories would make … and what power those stories would add to the supposedly staid and dreary image of a law practice.

At a blogging content workshop I gave recently, one of the breakout groups was working on blog ideas for a lawyer specialising in trust, wills and probate. Boring? No way. They came up with some wonderful ideas – many of them humorous – for example…

- Not letting the government take more than its fair share of your stuff when you die
- How to handle will making where there have been estrangements in a family
- How to deal with greedy relatives haggling over a will
- How to handle the difference between what you feel obliged to do and what you really want to do when making your will
- How to set up trusts so the beneficiaries don't get lazy
- …and many more.

They were extracting the human elements and stories from the seemingly dry and dusty legal topics. And that's the key here: it doesn't matter how dry and dusty the subject matter – it still affects humans.

Accountancy

Another person in the same workshop was an accountant and his elevator speech included the lovely line, "you have to pay the taxman, but you don't have to leave him a tip." Cue here, I suspect for some of the many taxman jokes that have been around for a long time, but if suitably edited and personalized would make a great "Jokes Corner" element on his blog.

As I have written about elsewhere, there's no harm in using humour in your business writing, provided that it's suitable for your audience and doesn't offend (although the taxman is fair game – even for taxmen...)

But accountancy will have some powerful human interest stories attached to it, too, not just "get your tax return in by next week" or "how to save and file all your receipts neatly." How about:

- Comfort for clients who hate keeping their own books
- Methods of handling your finances on a regular, frequent basis so it doesn't freak you out at the end of the financial year
- How to teach your kids to budget and handle their money
- The tactful ways to help seniors with their finances if they're no longer coping
- Tips on how to cut business or personal costs when cashflow is tight

- Firefighting tactics you need if you think your business is in trouble
- Etc...

Insurance

Large insurance companies cottoned on to the idea of powerful human interest stories to help sell their products a long time ago. I remember writing speeches for three senior insurance sales people at their company's annual convention in the Royal Albert Hall in London, England, whereby they had to speak for 20 minutes without notes or prompters and share their most memorable poignant human interest stories resulting from their having sold an insurance policy.

I wrote their speeches and coached them, even to the point of holding the hand of one speaker and literally leading her to the stage area because she was so scared. But through the day they told their stories. Each one of them got a standing ovation from 3,000 of their colleagues, many of whom were in tears. And the audience consisted only of more insurance sales people.

Moral of that story? Remember the words of our producer who, when I became nauseous after reading the schmaltzy human interest brief, said "If you want to get paid, write schmaltzy. Schmaltzy works."

It doesn't have to be schmaltzy, but you get the picture. Stories about people rescued from certain destitution by a wise insurance policy, a widow who was able to remain in her modest home to raise her children, a corpse which could be flown home from a far-flung location for a proper burial, etc... these stories – provided they're true - reach hearts and interest minds.

No matter how dry and unemotional your business or profession maybe, never forget that it affects people. And your readers will always identify with stories and information about people.

HUMOUR AND JOKES

Most people like a joke and a laugh, and every now and again a humorous blog post will lift your blogsite and get you some surprisingly good traffic, too, provided that you use an appropriate headline.

If you can, though, you should theme your humour to your business and to your readers' interests.

Should you want to have a try at writing bespoke jokes for your blogsite, I've added a few notes about it below. But if you haven't got the time or inclination…

Use Google to find jokes

Nearly all jokes have been around for years and no-one can remember who wrote the originals. Many are derivatives of earlier jokes, having been updated and adapted. As far as I am aware there can be no copyright on standard jokes for these reasons.

However, if you take a joke from a website you should say in your blog post where you got it from and include a link to that website.

And in any case, there's nothing to be ashamed of for the fact that you have curated some jokes from around the internet, carefully selected by you for your readers'/customers' entertainment. No-one will expect you to write jokes from scratch unless that happens to be what you do for a living.

So, to find some jokes about your area of business, do a Google search. Here are some examples of what I came up with:

Your business: landscape architect - I searched: jokes about gardening

- My wife said she's leaving me because of my unhealthy obsession with plants. I said where's this stemming from, petal?

- Gardening Rule: When weeding, the best way to make sure you are removing a weed and not a valuable plant is to pull on it. If it comes out of the ground easily, it is a valuable plant.

- New gardeners learn by trowel and error.

Your business: veterinary surgeon – I searched: veterinarian jokes

One day at the vet's surgery where I take my cat, a man and the receptionist were verbally sparring. After a few minutes a technician came to her co-worker's defence. "Sir," she asked the aggressive man, "do you know what happens to aggressive males in this surgery?"

Silly questions people ask their vet:

- My cat just came in from the garage and I was wondering...how many calories are in a mouse?
- I have a neutered male cat. How old should he be before I can breed him?
- What should I feed a borderline collie?
- What size litter box do I need to keep my cat comfy?
- Is it normal for a dog to shed?
- How can I keep my cat from stealing my husband's toothbrush?
- My cat passed a stool on the indoor rug and it's stuck in the vacuum cleaner. Any suggestions?
- How can I get the secret recipe for your special dog food?
- How do I stop my cat from giving food to the dog?
- Your food turned my dog into a stud. Now what do I do?
- Do you know how to toilet train a cat?
- I have three cats. Is it true that a special brand of cat food makes the poop smell better?
- Will chewing pop cans remove enamel from my puppy's teeth?
- Where can I get a six-toed cat?"

Your business: travel agent – I searched: travel jokes

- I had someone ask for an aisle seat so that their hair wouldn't get messed up by being near the window.
- A client called in inquiring about a package to Hawaii. After going over all the cost info, she asked, "Would it be cheaper to fly to California and then take the train to Hawaii?"

- I got a call from a woman who wanted to go to Capetown. I started to explain the length of the flight and the passport information when she interrupted me with "I'm not trying to make you look stupid, but Capetown is in Massachusetts. "Without trying to make her look like the stupid one, I calmly explained, "Capecod is in Massachusetts, Capetown is in Africa." Her response ... click.

- A man called, furious about a Florida package we did. I asked what was wrong with the vacation in Orlando. He said he was expecting an ocean-view room. I tried to explain that is not possible, since Orlando is in the middle of the state. He replied, "Don't lie to me. I looked on the map and Florida is a very thin state."

- I got a call from a man who asked, "Is it possible to see England from Canada?" I said, "No." He said "But they look so close on the map."

- Another man called and asked if he could rent a car in Dallas. When I pulled up the reservation, I noticed he had a 1-hour lay-over in Dallas. When I asked him why he wanted to rent a car, he said, "I heard Dallas was a big airport, and I need a car to drive between the gates to save time."

And so-on. It really is easy and a win-win all around as long as you credit your source.

How to tailor jokes for your own blog

Often you won't find a joke that's absolutely right for your blog and your readers. But there is a relatively simple way of tailoring jokes by adapting a core concept from one joke, and building another story around it that's relevant to your needs.

In this example, we use one core concept - the ridiculous notion that someone is so obsessed by his sporting interest that he will miss his own wife's funeral - which can be adapted to a number of different circumstances. Here are two examples ...

The Master and the Huntsman were leading a small mid-week field, trotting along a grass verge to the next covert. Along the road came a funeral cortege. The Huntsman pulled his horse up and took off his cap respectfully.

"I'm pleased to see you observe old-fashioned conventions, Hartley," said the Master, also pulling his horse up as hounds milled around expectantly. "Not many people have such good manners these days."

The Huntsman replaced his cap and prepared to move off again. "Thank you sir," he smiled. "But after all, we were married for twenty-eight years."

***

A golfer and his buddies were playing a big round of golf for $200. At the eighteenth green the golfer had a ten foot putt to win the round, and the $200. As he was lining up his putt, a funeral procession started to pass by.

The golfer set down his putter, took his hat off, placed it over his chest, and waited for the funeral procession to pass. After it passed, he picked up his putter and returned to lining up his putt, and completed it, thus winning the game and the money.

Afterwards, one of his buddies said, "That was the most touching thing I have ever seen. I can't believe you stopped playing, possibly losing your concentration, to pay your respects."

"Well," said the golfer, "we were married for 25 years."

You could adapt the same core concept and make the joke about many other outdoor sports and activities including soccer, baseball, football, lacrosse, field hockey, cross-country or marathon running, etc.

Shorter jokes that depend on a play on the words

A substantial proportion of the jokes you hear and see depend on a play on the words to provide the humour. With a little imagination you can use these as core concepts and adapt them so they're perfect for your readers.

Let's take a look at a few: I have emphasised the part of the joke that can be used as the core concept, around which you can substitute new circumstances to make the joke work in a different context (excerpted from The Horse Lover's Joke Book, by yours truly)…

The local Riding Club arranged a Christmas dinner for its large committee, but unfortunately the event was not up to much. One committee member complained to the Club Secretary.

*"**The food was awful**," he said. "Can you do something about it?"*

*"No," replied the Secretary. "You'll just **have to bring it up at the next** committee **meeting**."*

***

A young woman went to the doctor with a badly sprained ankle. The doctor strapped it up for her.

*"**Will I be able to** ride a horse **when it's better?**" she asked.*

"Of course you will," replied the doctor.

*"**That's odd**," said the woman. "**I've never** ridden a horse **in my life before.**"*

***

*The husband was complaining again. "**You're that absorbed in your** horses, **I'll bet you don't even remember** when we got married."*

*"**Of course I do**, darling,"* smiled his wife. *"**It was the day after** I won my first ever Medium test on Aurora."*

***

During a particularly spectacular pirouette in canter, the horse cast a shoe and it flew over a hedge, down a bank and out of sight. The horse and rider left the arena and went back to the yard, to find their instructor was there waiting to give a lesson to another livery owner. The rider told the instructor about the cast shoe and how it happened.

*"Aha," said the instructor. "Do you realize that shoe **went over the hedge, down the bank, on to the 4-lane highway below, and hit a motorcyclist hard on the head. He went out of control, a big truck and an RV swerved to miss him, collided, rolled over, and by the end of it 14 vehicles were involved and several people were injured."**

*"Oh, my God," said the rider, by now in tears and extremely distraught. "**What can I do? What can I do?"***
*The instructor thought carefully for a moment. "**In your shoes, I would use a little more** inside leg and shift your weight slightly further round on the outside seat bone."*

***

*The Head Girl in the riding school yard was furious as one of the working pupils **arrived late again**.*

"Angela," she yelled, *"**you should have been here at** half-past seven!"*

*"Why?" asked the pupil. "**What happened?"***

***

*The stable lad got his courage together and went to see the yard manager **to ask for a raise**. When he entered the office, the yard's **accountant was there too.** "I'd like a pay rise," stammered the young stable lad."*

*"Well, young man," said the accountant while the yard manager nodded wisely, "**due to the fluctuational predisposition of the global competitive equestrian economic climate as juxtaposed against the individual staff productivity within this particular enterprise, in my judgment I feel it would be fiscally inappropriate to elevate exponentially your specific increment."***

*"Yer what?" said the puzzled stable lad. "**I don't get it."***

*"**Exactly,"** said the yard manager.*

***

Just for fun, try and adapt one of the above jokes, substituting appropriate words, for your own readers:

I'll go first …

The wife was complaining again. "You're that absorbed in your business blogging and Social Media, I'll bet you don't even remember when we got married."

"Of course I do, darling," smiled her husband. "It was the day after I first joined LinkedIn."

Over to you!

IMAGES

No blogger can afford to ignore the importance of visual thinking. There is no way that one element of a blog post can be developed in isolation from the others: the internet is a multi-faceted, multi-media environment. In fact more now than ever before, words and pictures have got into bed with each other.

Video, too, has asserted itself as a keen blogging medium but this works more as a partner with text in blog posts, not usually as an illustration, although it can have that effect too. Essentially though as readers tend *either* to read the text *or* watch the video in a blog post (rather than glance at a still image while they're reading the text) video should be treated more as a standalone, though connected medium. See video section.

So what really can work as still images to support your blog posts?

Images? Do I need to draw?

No. All you have to do is broaden your scope out from the "words only" approach, and attune your mind to seeing your whole blog post (or other text issue) with all its elements as one overall concept.

And with a) a huge variety of free art and pictures on the internet plus b) the simplicity of taking good pictures of your own, sourcing great images is really easy. You just need to know what you're looking for.

Warning: a bad image is worse than no image at all

Too often I see blog posts in which the author has stuck a pretty picture which, although pretty, bears absolutely no relation to the blog's subject matter and therefore contributes nothing at all. If you can't find an image that adds something to your words, don't use one. Instead use bold cross-headings, pull quotes and other visual cosmetics to break up plain text and make your post more inviting to the eye.

Offensive images of any kind should be avoided, unless your blog post is about one of two things:

1. Drawing attention to some stark, shocking reality that your readers might not be aware of, e.g. the object of a charity fundraiser

2. A humorous subject, provided that your audience will find whatever scatological or other off-colour illustration you use to be genuinely funny

What images work best?

Images that work best, for me, pick up on points in the text – not necessarily the main points, but on points for which an illustration lifts their prominence and contribution to the post.

I personally love humour and even in serious posts, I'm attracted to images that pick up on points in at least a witty sort of way, if not in fall-about slapstick humour.

As long as you're careful not to stray over into areas of bad taste – e.g. using a humorous image in a post about death or illness – I think these slightly amusing illustrations help to lift the text and make the whole reading experience more entertaining.

What's more to the point, however, is to keep your images relevant without repeating what you're saying in the text, but rather using them to provide an extra dimension to it.

For example, if you're writing about brass screws, there's little point showing more than perhaps a thumbnail pic of a brass screw because everyone knows what they look like.

In this case, you need to use images that show why brass screws are better than steel ones … how much nicer they look when in place than other kinds … or perhaps a picture of them being made.

Where should they appear in the blog post?

Many blogging experts believe that you can use images to draw the reader's eyes into the text to begin with, then use subsequent ones to continue guiding their eyes onwards down to the end. Unless there are good reasons why not, you should try to alternate left-right-left-right so as to keep the flow going.

Where a picture shows a definite inclination to one side, always ensure that it inclines inwards towards the text – not away from it. With images not containing any text of their own, it's easy to "flip" the picture to whichever side you want using your Microsoft Office Picture Manager program or equivalent.

The importance of captions

I can't lay my hands on the science, but I do know that not only do pictures increase readers' interest and retention, but pictures with captions work even better. People love looking at pictures with words right there beside them, so it seems.

Whereas I'm not entirely convinced this is the case with blog posts, certainly I always try to include a caption under images *unless* the image itself contains words.

The captions can either be a relevant phrase or short sentence taken from the text, or – preferably – should be relevant but alternative words that link the image to your topic.

Where can I find good images for free?

I (and many of my blogging friends) use Stock.Xchng (http://www.sxc.hu/) which offers thousands of free images – be careful, however, to check their usage conditions as some require you to contact the photographer and gain permission, even though there is no charge.

Another good source that I use a lot is Photo Pin (http://photopin.com/) ... a huge database of "Creative Commons" images. Just be careful to tick the correct option when searching; if your site is in any way commercial, use only images from the commercial category. And then simply cut and paste the short lines of HTML on to the bottom of your post.

There are many more libraries of "free stock pictures" – have just Googled that phrase are there are more than 63 million results, so that should keep you going for a while!

What about original material?

Like most people these days I carry my phone around with me everywhere I go and I watch out for interesting signs, scenes, vehicles, etc. that might come in handy to illustrate a blog post one day.

Particularly if your blog is about a very specific topic or business, you are well placed to capture images that you know will work well to enhance your blog posts. Happy snapping!

Infographics

When infographics were first introduced they were heralded as the next best thing since sliced spam. I didn't warm to them and still haven't. Am I being weird? Does anyone else agree?

Here's Wikipedia's take:

Information graphics or infographics are graphic visual representations of information, data or knowledge intended to present complex information quickly and clearly. They can improve cognition by utilizing graphics to enhance the human visual system's ability to see patterns and trends. The process of creating infographics can be referred to as data visualization, information design, or information architecture.

Infographics to represent simple concepts like the weather forecast over the next few days have, as Wikipedia goes on to say, been around for a long time. But when we're talking somewhat more complex concepts I don't think they work as well, humans' visual systems seeing patterns and trends or not.

For a start, some infographics come in shapes that don't fit comfortably into your average desktop / laptop / tablet / smartphone screen formats. To read (and you have to read the words otherwise the pictures don't make sense) you need to scroll up and down quite a bit before you get the overall picture.

Many infographics are trailed in the social media and beyond with images so narrow there's no way you can read any of the information, visual or verbal, unless you click on the image once or more and eventually get to a size you can work with.

Biggest problem: it's the toy-toys again

When infographics first gained wide popularity a few years ago there was a rush of DIY kits on the market that provided you with infographic templates on a variety of different topics. All you had to do was personalize the information a little bit and voilà, instant blog post!

Trouble with that was yet again, putting the toy-toy cart before the content horse. In their rush to show off their exciting new format, newbie and even so-called "expert" bloggers totally forgot about what these things actually should be saying to their readers/customers and also, the importance of sharing information clearly and simply.

Creating your own infographic became a case of shoving nuggets of information in a pretty random order to match the cute pictures and icons, and to hell with what readers could take out of it if they even did manage to figure out what the underlying message was.

Quality infographics: built from scratch, by real experts

The infographic fans still rave about these vertical comic strips and of course, good ones that are properly designed and built from scratch are very effective.

But the DIY merchants who still try to express themselves with a format that can so easily become visually schizophrenic, are just asking for a mish-mashed message. And most likely they get either a mish-mashed response, or none at all.

Video

I've covered video elsewhere as it's quite a big topic in its own right. See Video section.

INTERVIEWS

You'd be surprised how many even quite famous people are happy to give interviews – probably because it's flattering to their egos! And if you pick the right characters within your industry area what they have to say will be of considerable interest to your readers/customers.

Interviews do not perform the same function as case histories, because they are not specifically about the interviewee's relationship with you and your company, although that might come into it if relevant.

Interviews are intended to share the interviewee's general wisdom, opinions on your business or industry area, advice to others in those areas, opinions on general topics that affect your industry or business area, visions for the future, etc.

Some potential interviewees for your blog

Obviously this depends a lot on what sort of business you're in, but here is a list of ideas to start you off:

Local, regional and national politicians – anyone from your local council or city governing body to your MP / Congressman etc. They will be able to contribute about local, regional or national trends in business and public sector management that could affect various different businesses in those areas. Make sure you keep your questions tight so they don't wander off into politic-speak that's not relevant...

Authors of books connected with your business area – keep a check on Amazon for any new books coming out that are relevant to your industry or business area and ask the author for an interview. Usually you can get hold of them by Googling the publisher's website, emailing their press office and asking for them to pass on your interview request to the author. If that doesn't work Google the author's name as they may have self-published and set up a website from which to sell the book, so you'll be able to contact them that way.

Local, regional and national experts – this can range from TV gardeners to university professors, depending on what you do. Don't be shy; often you'll think "oh, s/he would never take any notice of my blogsite" but in fact many of these people are a lot nicer than you think and will be glad to oblige! Once again, Google is your friend and should lead you to an appropriate contact pathway.

Journalists who specialize in your area – although most journalists are too busy to write guest posts for bloggers, they may well be willing to do either a vocal or email interview with you. This is particularly true for journos who work on smaller publications, trade press, etc. although you might be lucky and get an interview with a national figure, especially if your business is directly relevant to what they do.

Experts who are one step removed from your business area – these are people who wouldn't necessarily be your first choice but who nonetheless will have interesting things to say to your readers/customers. For example:

- A breast surgeon or nurse if your business sells bras and other lingerie
- A simultaneous translator if your business teaches a language
- A traffic policeman if you sell used cars

How to conduct interviews

These days some people are far too busy to take time out and be physically "interviewed" to provide quotes, information, testimonials, endorsements, etc.

And apart from the fact that to obtain a live face-to-face interview with someone (especially someone famous) takes more organizing than a nationwide military coup, you'll often find that the face-to-face variety isn't all that good anyway.

NB: If you do want to conduct an in-depth interview face-to-face or over Skype/FaceTime/Google Hangout etc., I have written a two-part tutorial on HTWB that you might like to read. It's too long and detailed (5,000 words) to include here in this book, but here are the links if you want to get the information:

Tutorial: how to interview like a pro business journalist (cut/paste, or copy, the links)

Part 1 - http://howtowritebetter.net/tutorial-how-to-interview-like-a-pro-business-journalist-part-1/

Part 2 - http://howtowritebetter.net/tutorial-how-to-interview-like-a-pro-business-journalist-part-2/

If you're short of time, though, what's the answer?

Email them the questions

This is not as simple as it sounds. People are a) busy and b) lazy, so if you want to get some good results you need to make it very, very easy for them to respond.

Naturally you need to establish that whoever you are to interview is happy with the arrangement. In the main you'll find that the prospect of their being able to answer questions in their own time, when it suits them, without an interviewer breathing down their neck, works for these people much better than any other alternative.

Arrange the eInterview first without asking any questions – just explain what you'd like to do and receive their agreement in principle.

Prepare your eInterview mail carefully. Write it out with a short introduction or recap on what you have agreed, then place your questions below. Embolden each question individually; if you embolden all questions in one sweep the response will come back in bold, too, which may make it hard for you to decipher. Be sure to remind them that all they have to do is hit return, key in their answers underneath each of your questions, then hit send.

The questions (Not too many...)

Essentially these should be focused on the old journalistic principles of "who, what, where, when and how," with appropriate modification. But here's a warning; don't overdo the number of questions. People are put off on email if there is a long list

Let's say you're looking to obtain a good testimonial for a client (alter appropriately if the project is to get a testimonial for your own business). Here's a list of questions from another article of mine which should give you a good spread of quotes, but select only 5 or 6 or them if you don't want to scare your interviewee off:

- What is it that you think makes XXX different from their competitors?
- Just how much better than the competition do you feel XXX really is?
- Why do you feel that XXX is more efficient than other, similar (whatever)?
- How would you rate your experience of working with/using XXX?

- Compared with their competitors, how do you rate your experience of working with/using XXX?
- On a 1 to 10 scale, how would you rate your experience of working with/using XXX, and why?
- What difference has using XXX made to your business's/department's performance?
- What is it about XXX's performance/service that makes the different?
- What was it that made you choose XXX in the first place?
- What was it that made you choose XXX instead of their competitors?
- What was it that made you change from your previous (whatever) to XXX?
- What additional benefits have you found through using XXX?
- What are the three main benefits of working with XXX?
- In summary, then, what would you say is the key benefit of working with XXX?
- In summary, then, what difference has working with/using XXX made to your bottom line?
- How important is it to you that you should work with/use XXX in the future?
- What sort of future do you think XXX can look forward to?
- If I were someone considering using XXX, what advice would you give me?

And for some more general questions?

When you're doing an email interview with someone to obtain information that's not necessarily an endorsement or testimonial, you need to research the topic a little bit more thoroughly and plan whatever it is you're going to write, so that your email interview questions run alongside your plan and so lead to providing you with the information you need.

For example, let's look at an email interview about the need for businesses to employ a truly professional recruitment agency: here are the questions I would ask of the recruitment agency head honcho for a blog post aimed at his/her potential clients:

- To what extent do you feel that the recruitment process for managers is a continuous cycle, rather than a linear process?

- What are the benefits to a client company of hiring a recruitment agency as opposed to setting up and internal recruitment function?

- In your experience, what are the most important criteria for a client to consider when selecting a recruitment agency, in order of importance, and why?

- How should a client company in this sector go about the process of selecting an agency?

- At selection stage, what should the client company expect the agency to do in terms of research and information-seeking?

- Once the agency is selected, what are the most important elements to incorporate into the formal appointment? (E.g. contract, T&Cs, length of agreement, timing of reviews, termination terms, etc., but especially anything over and above what a client company would ordinarily expect)

Assessing your results and using them

Much as people might tell you that interviewing by email doesn't result in such thorough responses as you might get from the F2F variety, it's not necessarily true.

Invariably the results I get from these emailed interview questions are good because a) the responses are relatively short and sweet which for contemporary online purposes is what we need, and b) the fact that people have time to think about what they're going to respond with enables them to do it better than they would "off the cuff."

So in conclusion, eInterviews can work and are a very acceptable alternative to the F-2-F variety.

The choice is yours!

JARGON BUSTING AS A BLOG TOPIC

There must be very, very few businesses, industries and other commercial concerns that haven't developed at least a few terms of their own jargon.

Depending on how much jargon exists in your own business area, a "jargon buster" piece could be anything from a one-off blog post to a series running to several articles.

Obviously all such jargon must be that with which your readers have to deal, but from there on you are working to an open brief.

How to define jargon

You know your readers, so you need to adjust your definitions of your business's jargon appropriately. That won't be hard for you.

Think about the terms you and your colleagues use every day, and how they might impact on your readers.

Are they really as self-explanatory as they seem to you, or would they perhaps cause confusion for someone not familiar with your business?

What jargon to describe

It goes without saying that the jargon you write about in your blog posts should be that which your readers are likely to come up against in their dealings with you and the service/products you provide.

If you're not sure how to go about defining your business's jargon, here's an idea that would be useful all around…

Ask your best customer to help you out here

Sort out a list of the terms relating to your business which are most likely to confuse your readers, then ask one of your favourite customers to do an "interview" with you.

This option could even result in a humorous post which is even more likely to capture your readers' attention.

Never mind the laughs: jargon matters

I know I shouldn't laugh at jargon as much as I do because it forms a key part of many people's working lives.

And where you can provide some very helpful jargon-busting information within your own industry, profession or business, you will be doing your readers/customers a big favour. Go for it!

JARGON, USING IT

Jargon is a close relative of clichés and acronyms but is sometimes more difficult to avoid, especially when you're writing to technically literate readers who use the jargon terms as much as you do and know what they all mean.

Unwanted jargon, specialized terms and other business babble, however, can turn up in all sorts of places, including blogs - not just technical documents and presentations.

If you're putting together a company sales meeting, for example, you might sit up until midnight with the engineering people winkling all the jargon out of their boss's speech on new product specifications, only to find that on the day the finance director does 20 minutes of figures and computations full of financial jargon that not even the CEO understands.

Marketing and advertising people are prone to jargonitis too. FMCG and market segmentation may seem perfectly understandable terms to them but will go over the salesforce's heads – not a good idea if your marketing director is trying to wow them with enthusiasm in a blog post about the new corporate ad campaign that's going to have their customers gagging to buy more from them.

People will often tell you that you can't remove jargon from business communication like blogs without seriously "dumbing it down," but don't believe a word of it. It is possible to make almost any topic understandable to any reasonably intelligent audience without insulting that intelligence. It just takes a bit more effort and thought.

Bloggers who hide behind jargon

And that brings me neatly to another point to be wary of: people, especially less-than-adequate people who blog, love to hide behind jargon and other gobbledy-gook. It's part of that old line about "blinding them with science" and is closely related to the pompous-speak so loved by producers of corporate literature and online text.

In a similar way, using jargon and technical terms makes these people feel important and in control, especially when their readers don't understand what they're talking about but feel too intimidated to say so.

Not only is that incredibly rude to the readers concerned, but it's also dangerous. For example, if the person writing the blog isn't really an expert and is using the jargon wrongly, it won't be long before someone realizes and bursts out laughing – not good for business.

So does jargon have any advantages?

The main advantage I can see about jargon is that it saves time and cuts out a lot of lengthy explanations. Provided you're sure that your readers understand it all, your blog will be substantially shorter than if you wrote out every term in full. If you're unsure about your readers' level of technical literacy but still want to use jargon they may not understand, a useful solution is to provide them with a short glossary of the jargon, acronyms, abbreviations etc. as a click through page on your blog.

KNOW-HOW

Informative, authoritative blog posts are very valuable. But too much knowhow can put readers off if it's dry, dull and boring.

No worries, however; there are ways to lighten the load and make these posts more appealing.

Having proofread my son's university essays (on econometrics) recently I am still reeling from being engrossed in text that is more dense than a Brazilian rain forest. Of course, academic writing has to be like that and I assume the tutors, lecturers and other staff are well used to wading through the treacle of words that students write.

But out here in the real world, readers – your customers and prospects – don't have the time or inclination to absorb information to anything even remotely like that degree of intensity. That's why any information-based blog post you write needs to allow plenty of breathing space around facts and figures, interspersing the solid information with lighter interludes that allow readers to catch their breath.

Some ways to introduce a lighter note into information-heavy text

Case studies

These are very effective ways of providing two useful things: one, a diversion from the fact-packed main text, and two, where relevant, emphasis on the part you played in the success story. Be sure to keep case studies in blog posts pretty short and sweet, and link as often as possible to how the good stuff in the case study can apply to you-the-reader, as well. If you want to use longer case studies, offer the long version as a download or link through to it elsewhere on your blog or website, and just use a snappy summary of the key points in your blog posts. You want to keep your blog post moving.

Stories

These aren't the same as case studies because you can always make them up if one doesn't immediately spring to mind! Business storytelling is very fashionable right now. I confess I feel wee bit cynical when I read about yet another rags to riches story or how someone tripping over a dandelion sparked off a million-selling business idea or how a little boy's Lego structure inspired the highest skyscraper in the Middle East … you get the drift. Stories are great but in a business context, leave out the sob-stuff, gnomes and fairies at the bottom of the garden, and focus on lightish relevance.

Humour

See more about humour and jokes in the Humour and Jokes section, but for now…

- By all means include a joke, but make sure it's tailored to your readers and their interests
- If your readers include people for whom English is a second language, it's probably best to avoid jokes
- For all audiences, use humour sparingly … as a "condiment" rather than as a main course
- Unless you're certain your readers can handle a bit of naughtiness, keep your humour squeaky-clean

Images

The old cliché about a picture being worth a thousand words became a cliché, as most do, because it's absolutely true and valid across the board. By breaking up your text with images you give the reader some sensory relief (NLPers would back me up here, I think…) and images can achieve a lot more than merely offering pretty pictures. See the images section.

LOCAL BUSINESS BLOGGING

There is a lot of excitement going on in cybercircles at the moment about online marketing for local businesses, but many local businesses don't yet see how blogging can work for them and their customers / prospects.

First of all, let's establish what we mean by "local businesses." My interpretation, at least, is businesses where the vast majority of their customer bases are within a relatively confined geographical area. And by implication, this would suggest businesses that function primarily offline to deliver their products and services. Some, although not all, are likely to fall into the SME or even solopreneur categories.

Here are a few examples that I can think of:

- Plumbing and heating
- Electrical contracting
- Law and accountancy firms
- Taxis and personal transport
- Automotive retailing
- Wealth management
- Book-keeping
- Hospitality, restaurants, resorts, conference facilities

- Complementary therapies
- Franchise holders (various)

First the bad news

Even if your locality is in a city or other densely populated area, realistically you are not going to attract a readership of thousands, although as some of your blog posts will be about generic things which appeal to everyone in your business area you might get lucky!

But here more than almost anywhere in the business blogosphere, readers for your blog posts are all about quality, not quantity. You may not be getting over a thousand visits a day to your website, but even if you get just 20 good ones, don't worry. Your conversion rate is likely to be a lot higher than that of any of your competitors who don't blog, or who blog badly/irregularly/etc.

A local business has a "small but perfectly formed" readership

The good news about that bad news is because you're dealing with a geographical locality that you know well already, you're far more likely to know where to look for new customers and prospects than if you're blogging even nationally, never mind internationally.

That narrows your field down considerably and although your audiences may be on the small side, there'll be little "wastage" (i.e.

people reading your blog who for whatever reason couldn't possibly buy from you.)

It should also be relatively easy to build up a subscription list of good, convertible prospects - especially if you co-ordinate your blogging activities with face-to-face business networking in your locality.

Don't forget, also, that there are many apps available for advertising and promoting local businesses on mobile and other devices, as well as various LinkedIn and to a lesser extent Facebook and Google Plus groups based around a business locality in which you can participate and promote your blog.

Combine both "local" and "business" for a really sharp focus in blog posts

Depending on the nature of your business, you can combine your own local knowledge with your business expertise to the benefit of your readers. By keeping abreast of local business and other news, you can write blog posts that home right in on key issues that affect everyone in the area.

For example...

- Local weather issues (e.g. flooding and tree falls)
- New motorway / highway planned through locality
- Housing shortages / developments
- Local business award schemes, new business networking groups, apprenticeships, recruitment

- Interviews with key local figures who have an effect on your readership
- Local sports facilities and activities
- Upcoming exhibitions and other events in the area
- Local motoring news, traffic issues
- Local retail activities, new store openings, fashion, shopping, hair, beauty, spa resources, etc.
- A jobs page listing vacancies relevant to your business within your locality

You need to ensure that whatever local issue you write about links strongly to your own business and your customers and prospects, however - don't just be another local business news source!

Put your own stamp on each issue and invite discussion about it from your readers - brilliant for making your blog "sticky" and retaining reader loyalty.

So if your business is all about local, don't think that a blog isn't worth doing. Provided that you write about the right things it really will make a huge difference to your business's online and offline brand image - plus it will gain you respect and a following you'll find invaluable.

NEWS AND CURRENT AFFAIRS AS BLOG TOPICS

Before we move on to the daily papers, it's worth mentioning news feeds here. These can be set to provide you with a stream of information relating to your business, topic or whatever, and as such is a useful way of keeping in touch with what is going on in your industry.

I don't, however, think they can replace the more original, interesting ideas that will get triggered in your mind when you scan over the general news media.

Bookmark all the relevant news media

With a little research you can find and bookmark newspaper and other publications' websites not only in your own country, but of course almost anywhere in the world. Here's a checklist to start you off...

Local media – particularly important if you work and blog locally, of course. Newspapers are an obvious choice as are local radio stations, most of which are likely to have mailing lists you can join for updates, news feeds, and also Twitter feeds which are probably the quickest way to keep up with what's going on locally from day to day.

National media – for the main news and views from your country's perspective. Most national newspapers have websites that provide very up to date information not just on general news, but on more specific topics like science, health, fashion, food, finance and so-on. Explore these media carefully and bookmark any pages that could possibly link to your own topic or business.

International media – if you do business with other countries – or your customers do - get on to Google and search for their national newspapers. Many countries in which English is not the main language will still have an English language newspaper and/or news website, so if you don't speak the foreign language search for (e.g.) Brazil+"English language newspapers".

Specialized/trade media – as with other print publications many specialized and trade magazines have accompanying websites and they can be goldmines for information and ideas for your blog posts. You probably know the best ones in your topic area, so get them bookmarked and get on their updates lists, Twitter feeds, etc.

Set up Google Alerts

Google Alerts are wonderful things … they allow you to be informed about specific topics and issues, bringing in links by email for you both from the web and from the news media. Here's what they say you can have:

*"**Monitor the Web for interesting new content**
Google Alerts are email updates of the latest relevant Google results (web, news, etc.) based on your queries. Enter a search query you wish to monitor. You will see a preview of the type of results you'll receive. Some handy uses of Google Alerts include:*

- *monitoring a developing news story*
- *keeping current on a competitor or industry*
- *getting the latest on a celebrity or event*
- *keeping tabs on your favourite sports teams"*

You can choose from a variety of search choices in the drop-down menus, and have as many Alerts on the go as you want, all at the same time.

And best of all, the service is free.

Those two activities should keep you abreast of everything going on within your industry … and even news that isn't directly connected with your business may well trigger an idea for a blog post in your mind.

OPINIONS

Opinions are like tomatoes: delicious and welcome when they're ripe and plump, but utterly undesirable if they are rotten or don't fit in with a particular menu.

So how should we incorporate opinions – our own, as well as others' – into our blog posts? Should we insulate them with get-out clauses that compensate for any potential disagreement, or should we say what we think in a carefree, gung-ho manner and the hell with the consequences?

Or should we adopt a journalistic stance and stick purely with the facts when we're writing blog posts?

First catch your buffalo, as we Canadians say

Before you decide on whether or not to share your own personal opinion in a blog post, I think it's important that you lay out the facts of the topic for your readers to consider first of all.

I know that sometimes it's good to smack your readers across the face with a controversial thought or argument, but if you're in business and want to maintain your kudos as someone knowledgeable in your field, to strike out with an opinion upfront will seem arrogant and possibly, even, conceited.

Before you go into your opinions, no matter how strongly you feel about the issue concerned, present a factual case for readers to consider.

Then start a new section (with a new cross heading) and express your own opinions on the issue. Finally, round off by asking your readers what they think, and invite them to share their views in the comments.

What about others' opinions?

If you want to turn your blog post into a true discussion it's worth finding out what key people and even "gurus" in your industry think about the issue and incorporating their views in your text. You can do this in one of two ways:

1. **Google the topic and check out what the industry leaders are saying about it.** Set up a Google Alert using the topic's keywords and wait until you get some useful feedback – providing your topic isn't too obscure you will get feedback pretty soon. (As I mentioned earlier, the Google Alert service is free ... for now, anyway!)

2. **Find and contact thought leaders on this topic and ask them for their views.** Despite being perpetually "busy" a lot of these people are happy to answer quick questions and all you need for your blog post is one or maybe two quotes. If you get in there, email the person you choose with a question or two to which s/he can respond simply by hitting

"reply" and slotting their answer in after your question. It takes very little time and you'll be surprised by the helpful responses you might get, even from famous types.

Using opinions as a discussion pivot

Although I've mentioned asking readers' views in the comments, you can take this a bit further and ask some of your key readers or customers what their views are on the topic before you write the post (letting them know that you will be using their input and asking if they want to be attributed with a link to their business URL or, to remain anonymous.)

This way you can incorporate a range of different viewpoints and approaches to your topic in your original post. The advantage here is that the fact that your post already contains a number of different people's opinions, it will attract further discussion more fluently than if you ask people simply to share their views on what you think alone.

And don't be afraid of conflicting opinions

Unless you view your blog purely as a sales platform for you and your business (and please Heavens that you don't) you should be brave enough to incorporate opinions that don't necessarily chime with your own.

Why? Because you can acknowledge the fact that we can agree to differ, and more importantly you can use such differing views to create a stimulating discussion that allows you to show your expertise in countering the dissenter's views, and showing him/her as well as all other readers that you really do know what you're talking about.

PASSION

A number of people I know in some businesses - mainly those connected with personal, spiritual, intellectual and other more cerebral issues - write blog posts or articles in an incredibly powerful, passionate way ... which hits you in the face with its value and earnestness.

If, that is, you can grasp their key points right away.

Trouble is, in the flurry of passion within which those thoughts try to emerge, the average reader can't necessarily grasp just how important – or where - the key points are.

So, passionate experts: take note...

Passion, power and practical usability: not a perfect mix

The whole blogging phenomenon has given passionate bloggers/writers the opportunity to share their views in writing without the threat of an editor lurking with a blue pencil to change their words and water down their enthusiasm, albeit in the name of clarifying vagaries and making the text easily absorbed by the masses.

For followers of such bloggers and like-minded readers, these rushes of densely-packed words are comprehensible and share the high levels of emotion that drive their inspiration.

However where does that leave the less-than-imaginative readers who would love to benefit from the passionate ideas … but don't necessarily follow the rapid, often turbulent, trains of thought?

And how many opportunities are these passionate writers losing because readers who would like to learn from them, follow them and possibly buy from them, don't "get" their messages as quickly as they need to in this rapid-fire online culture we live in?

Harness your passion with a few straps of simplicity

As I mentioned above, many of the passionate bloggers and article writers I know are sharing some incredibly good, worthwhile knowledge and recommendations. But by the nature of their passionate style, they are potentially losing out on readership and business from the wider marketplace.

My advice to these writers here is, learn how to relax your thoughts into an article or post that sets out those thoughts in a logical manner.

I know, I know. Logical stodge does not sit well with passionate expertise. But relax: it *is* possible to combine those two elements without diluting the force of your convictions or the intelligence of your content.

Some suggestions to make your writing passionate, powerful *and* practical

Plan your article before you start writing. Remember how you would plan your essays at university? That gives you a brief skeleton to follow so your article has a logical beginning, middle and end. Don't just start writing and rush your thoughts down, because although they may seem in an order that's logical to you, that may not be true for all your readers. Work to a plan.

Use punctuation properly – it's a valuable tool. People yawn when you talk about punctuation but used correctly it adds a huge amount of power to your written content. Use it to clarify what you mean. This article by novelist Lucy McCarraher in her HTWB series "How To Write Fiction Without The Fuss" gives you some very helpful tips on punctuation for nonfiction, too. Check it out here – http://howtowritebetter.net/how-to-write-fiction-without-the-fuss-the-beauty-of-good-punctuation/ (or go to the site and key "punctuation" into the search box top right.)

Avoid exclamation marks, underlining, capitals, etc. Much as I know how tempting it is to use typographical emphasis when writing about something I feel passionate about, in the cold light of day readers think it looks tacky. By all means use these tricks when you're writing your draft, but go back and chop them out when you edit (see below).

Particularly when you are writing online, simplify sentences. Make sure you use a separate sentence for each whole thought – you can use colons to separate long clauses (see punctuation, above) but online it's better to spread your thoughts out more widely. Make each sentence lead logically into the next … each paragraph lead logically into its successor.

Avoid all but very short parentheses. Whether you use brackets or dashes, keep them to a minimum. There are enough distractions in the online environment as it is without adding another few into the equation. Try to keep your readers focused on the key point you're making in the main sentence, so their attention keeps on the right track.

Online, use very short paragraphs. There's something about the online environment that makes long blocks of text look very uninviting – far more so than do long blocks of text in print. Keep your paragraphs to a maximum of five sentences: fewer is better. And, vary the length of your sentences; follow two or three long sentences with one short one. Keeps readers on their toes.

Make use of sub-headings and bold titling. I use these to break up the text visually and also to "tell the story" to readers who, as many online readers do, scan through articles and posts before settling down to read them properly. You may find you can develop these from the plan you work out before starting on the writing.

Edit your text, but don't strangle it. Many literary fiction editors tell you to cut, cut, cut and then cut again, strip out all but essential adjectives and adverbs, etc. I disagree with that notion in nonfiction blog writing, because if you edit a piece too hard you'll strip out the writer's personality along with everything else. By all means remove or correct any unnecessary duplication, fuzzy or vague statements, convoluted thoughts and of course, typos and other glitches. But don't lose yourself.

Take a break before you publish. Leave your article or post for a few hours or overnight if you can. A break from it will give you a fresh focus and help you make more effective improvements. No matter how much I think an article of mine is OK once I have finished it, if I leave it until later or the next day I always find improvements to be made.

So remember: practicality ... ergo, simplification ... does not mean dumbing-down. It merely means that your passionate and powerful thoughts are subject to a little bit more discipline, which allows readers to absorb your information and emotions faster and more thoroughly.

PROMOTING YOUR BLOG POSTS

Once you've written your business blog, you have to promote it. Otherwise how will anyone else other than your Mom and your dog know it's out there and of interest to your readers?

This is where many bloggers crumble and feel that to promote their wise words across the internet is like boasting / bragging and really is shameful. I have one word to say to that:

Bullsh*t.

If you're in business, you have every right to promote your business blog. In fact, business sense says that you must.

You do this via your mailing list and other direct contacts and connections you may have, but above all, you do it via Social Media.

No doubt you're already involved with a number of social media (SocMed) platforms like Facebook and LinkedIn. Depending on your particular industry, some of the SocMed sites are going to be more useful to you than others.

Here are some tips on how I promote my posts/articles/tutorials on some of the SocMed sites ...

Facebook

If you have a business page on Facebook, you'll find that its reach has been restricted quite severely due, no doubt, to FB wanting to increase the monetizing of its activities. Bottom line: you need to pay to get your business page posts viewed beyond a very small percentage of your followers.

Meanwhile when sharing posts and articles on your FB business page, make sure you link correctly to the places concerned.

And always write a lead-in ... something to accompany your posts – an explanation, a short introduction or other quip – if you don't want them to look like spam.

Google Plus

As far as I can understand it there are no real restrictions on how you promote your blog posts as public shares on Google Plus provided, of course, that they are credible, decent and offer some value. Be sure to hashtag them appropriately. I try to avoid using more than two or maximum three hashtags as otherwise the post begins to look a bit like a three-ring circus.

Where your post may well attract more traffic is from various communities allied to what you do, but be careful: many communities have strict rules about what you can and can't post, so do check first their rules first if you don't want to get banned.

As with Facebook, always write a lead-in to whatever you post, and if you post the same article to more than one community as well as the "public" variety, ensure that each lead-in is different. People don't want to read stuff posted by robots.

One great advantage Google Plus offers at the time of writing this (mid 2014) is a WordPress plugin that automatically **transfers all comments on a blog post you promote, back into the comments section of your blog** (as well, of course, as remaining on Google Plus.) And the system works both ways; you can comment on the G+ section of comments on your own blog, add "plus ones," etc. and they will all come up in both places. Genius!

LinkedIn

Once again I don't think there are any hard and fast rules about what you can share on LinkedIn apart from the obvious restrictions of decency, relevance and value.

With the LinkedIn audiences being so very business focused, however, you need to make sure your post is not only relevant to a business audience but of a sufficiently sophisticated standard to meet that business audience's criteria.

As with the other SocMed platforms a good lead-in is helpful, but as my good friend and fellow networker Mark Orr says about people posting on LinkedIn, "My own policy is not to click on the link in any discussion post in LinkedIn that doesn't have some detail in it beyond the simple headline. I would like the person posting to invest a little more of their time helping me to make an informed judgment about investing my own time in (reading) their post."

Mark is right! So be sure to use your lead-in to suggest "what's in it for you" for people if you want them to read your new post.

And if that leads to a conversation about your topic right there and then on Linked In, **it doesn't necessarily have to stay there.** If it happens within a public forum or group, it's OK to cut it and paste it into a comment slot on your own blog. If it takes place within a closed or private group, ask the other participants for their permission to share it with your own blog. You'll find that most participants are happy for this to happen, especially if you include links to their business pages and/or websites.

Twitter

Here we have a different ballgame. But even within 140 characters there can still be room to create some sort of brief come-hither words, even after the post title, as hashtags. Unless your blog post headline suggests a benefit for readers, consider using a few extra words in your tweet that hint at what readers will get from clicking on through.

StumbleUpon

StumbleUpon is very sweet, precious and middle class American … it doesn't like naughty words or thoughts. Just recently it rejected a share from me by saying words to the effect of "you can't share any more posts here today" when in fact it turned out their real problem with it was that the headline contained the word "whiskey," and I had categorized the post as "safe for work."

As soon as I retried without using the dreaded Prohibition word, all was sweetness and light again. Be conscious of this prissiness and word your lead-in and keywords appropriately…

Pinterest

With Pinterest you need to pick and choose. Bearing in mind their demographic, the heaviest-weight business articles are unlikely to attract much attention. Much as so-called "social media experts" proclaim that Pinterest is a good platform for business of all kinds, my own experience and understanding is that yes, OK, but realistically if you blog about plumbing tools in Poland or fish gutting in New Brunswick, Pinterest ain't the platform for you.

If your product or service is attuned to the Pinterest mainstream readership – especially across the visual and other creative arts, retail, luxury goods, weddings, cooking and gastronomy, sports, writing, health, etc. etc. – by all means post and you'll get some interest. Be sure that your illustration is good, too, or your post won't attract much attention.

With Pinterest I always share a good lead-in and make it clear that the picture isn't everything, usually by writing "…read on!" at the end of the lead-in.

More blog post promotion ideas

Use your email list. If you do a newsletter to your list, make sure you tell recipients about your blog. Depending on the frequency of your posts and your email newsletters, you can even send out an email alert each time a new post goes live on your blog, containing a short "taster" paragraph to encourage readers to click through to your site to read the whole article. Encourage recipients to share the news about your blog posts with friends and colleagues.

Use your Facebook business page to post links to your most recent blog posts. Join relevant business groups on Facebook and share those links with them. Register your blog on NetworkedBlogs to attract more traffic.

With Facebook, LinkedIn and Google Plus you can also **set up your own groups** (called "communities" on Google Plus) where you can share your own material and also curate other articles etc. of interest to your audience.

Also consider using bookmarking sites like StumbleUpon, Digg, Reddit, etc.

Guest blogging on other people's blogs is always a good way to spread the word about your own. Your direct competitors may not be too keen to invite you to guest blog for them!! However you may find there are a number of sites whose business activities are allied to your own and for whom you could provide specialized expertise. So check them out, contact them and ask. Be sure when you submit your post that you're given a short bio at the end with a link to your new blog.

Get guest bloggers for your blog. Provided that you let guest posters include a bio and a link to their own sites, they will benefit from the extra publicity they'll get if they guest for you. If you're just starting out, however, people might not be willing to spend the time given that your audience is going to be small to begin with. Instead you might like to try interviewing them − see the Interviews section for tips on how to do that successfully. The interviewees are still likely to promote the post as they won't have had to do much work for it!

Commenting on other people's blog posts, provided your comments are useful and constructive, is another good way to spread you and your blog's presence around.

Business cards and other printed material. If your blog is going to be your main online presence, be sure that its URL is clearly included on all your printed business stationery.

Your email sig file. Don't forget to make the most of this small sales opportunity ... include your blog's URL in your signature file, along with your contact details.

Don't overdo the promotion of your blog posts in Social Media

Much as your blog posts may be relevant and of interest to readers on Facebook, Twitter, etc., readers will become resentful if all you ever do is stuff your own content in their faces. Be sure to balance your blog post shares with other useful information that helps – not sells to – your audiences.

QUESTIONS AND ANSWERS, AS A BLOG POST

Questions and answers are often a good format to get information across in a way that suggests input from outsiders, to which you supply answers that cordially address their particular problems and offer them, and others, your way of thinking and so invite them into your potential client base.

No-one in business is naïve enough to think that the average written Q&A session is made up solely of genuine questioners asking genuine questions. The Q&A section of most business documents and online presences is nearly always made up of the questions you'd like customers and prospects to ask, and the answers you'd like to give them.

This is not really as dishonest and slimy as some might think: there is nothing whatsoever wrong with posing typical customer questions in your blog posts, and answering them honestly. But…

So where should these questions come from?

Ideally, real queries from real customers / clients. But if those are not forthcoming in writing, don't worry: you are very likely to know the type of questions your customers are likely to ask, and should be able to pre-empt such questions easily.

If you're not confident that you know what sort of questions your customers may ask, go and ask them. A research exercise on your part asking customers what their prime business concerns are and how suppliers like you should be able to help them, is something you should be doing anyway. And all the more so if what you find out from them is going to result in information that helps everyone – you and your customers included.

How do you use questions and answers?

The most obvious place, first of all, is the Frequently Asked Questions page on your website. (You do have one, I hope?!!) No-one will be surprised to find that you may manipulate this page to suit your marketing purposes, and to a certain extent that's OK.

But whatever you do, please avoid the temptation to use it as a means of glorifying your business unrealistically. Questions like this (and trust me, you do see them…) are ridiculously wrong:

- Why is it that you're the leading electrical contractors in (name of town)?
- You've convinced me. How can I get in touch with you in the fastest way possible?

- Should I ignore all other (types of business) in (name of town) considering that your firm is so well qualified?
- …etc. Yuk.

Another way to use questions and answers effectively is in blog posts, and the same criteria apply here.

Never mind questions about you: focus on issues your customers may have

Whether it's in an article / blog post on your website or in the FAQ page of your website, you'll gain far more "brownie points" and engagement from your readers if the "questions" are angled entirely at invoking answers that a) show you know your stuff generically (essential if you want to be credible) and that b) prove the benefits of using your services to achieve the associated aims.

Don't get these two wrong, or in the wrong order. If you do, you lose your readers' interest.

Technical questions

If your business has a technical element, a Q and A section and format for blog posts may well be very helpful.

But not all readers – especially the decision makers who buy from you ultimately - will want to know the precise inside leg measurement of a small gnat just emerging from puberty.

Bear in mind who your customers / clients really are, and focus your questions and answers on them.

Make sure that ultra-techies can find out what you're about by clicking on through to another page on your website that includes the information they need.

Remember that your readers – potential customers – are, except in rare circumstances, unlikely to be as technically literate as you and your boffins are.

Write your blog posts for average humans and box off the techie bits for boffins separately.

RANTS

Do you ever get so annoyed about something in business that you just have to write it all down in a blog post? Something that makes you seethe with rage so much you simply can't wait to share it with your readers and customers?

Certainly, a lively rant is attention grabbing

Even if you manage to leave out the swearwords, shouting your anger via a blog post will certainly grab the attention of your readers and anyone else who happens to come across your post via SocMed or other networking platform.

But you need to watch you don't grab attention for the wrong reasons

To begin with, be very conscious of defamation laws (see the expert's view below). No matter how justified you may feel in doing a thorough demolition job on a company or individual, their lawyers might not agree with you. Don't buy yourself trouble that you don't need.

Bear in mind that some companies and business people might even see an occasion like this as an opportunity to launch a lawsuit which will gain them publicity and possibly even a lot of your money, too.

Never publish your rant when you're angry

...or if you've had a few drinks to calm yourself down. You'd be surprised at how cringe-making you can find an article or post the next morning, when the night before you thought it was the best thing you have ever written. Use the cold, harsh light of day to help you edit out the libellous bits.

Many psychologists and counsellors advise you to write a letter to or article about someone expressing your anger / hurt / frustration / resentment / etc. as a means of getting it off your chest. You're then expected to delete the whole thing, which strikes me as a waste of time.

If you're that p*ssed off it's more productive to go mow the lawn or vacuum clean your house. Those will work off your anger and be useful as well.

If you feel you genuinely need to share your rant

Once you've cooled off about it and given it a bit of time, you may still feel you should share your unfortunate experience with your readers and customers, as they might benefit from the warning. This is when you should examine your article carefully for legal tripwires and tone down any strong language.

You need to check this with your legal adviser, but as far as I can see it you are entitled to express your own personal opinion online about pretty much anything you want. Where the problems can arise is when you suggest or state derogatory things about a person or company unless, of course, it is true. And ideally, you should be able to provide evidence that it's true.

The expert's view

"When things get heated it may feel like a natural reaction to lash out and tell a business exactly what you think but do be careful not to find yourself on the receiving end of a defamation claim," says **Steph Barber** *of the UK's popular* **Law Hound online legal services firm****. *"Defamation is a word which covers both libel (something more permanent so a written blog, but also images or other electronic media and broadcasts or links) and slander (more transient such as speech)."*

"The law of defamation doesn't give us a single definition of what would actually be defamatory but instead, will consider your post taking into account "the estimation of right-thinking members of society generally". So, taking a common sense approach, avoid posting anything which is likely to:
* discredit the business or any individuals within it
* make people think worse of them
* lower them in the estimation of others
* mean that they are avoided, shunned or exposed to ridicule, contempt or hatred
...by those "right-thinking members of society generally"

"In reality, it means that you really need to think carefully about what you post. However, the law of defamation is currently undergoing

changes and so a business will have to prove that a defamatory statement has caused or is likely to cause them serious financial loss, but, if they can for example, show a loss of orders, this may not be so difficult to prove. For a micro business that has no accounts to show and few clients, it's much harder to make a case."

"There are defences available to any potential claim so, for example, you could rely on a defence of honest opinion, provided you meet the criteria. However, remember that a court will take an objective view."

Please bear in mind that this advice is based on UK law - laws in other countries may vary, but the basic principles are likely to be similar.

** go to http://www.lawhound.co.uk

READERS' EMERGENCIES AS BLOG TOPICS

This one shouldn't be difficult for you because chances are you deal with your customers' emergencies already and very efficiently too! However you want to remind them of how knowledgeable you are and also to reassure prospective customers or clients that you have the know-how to deal with any issue that might arise as and when they put their business your way.

Truly big-time emergencies really don't need too much emphasis in your blog, because it's implicit that you're capable of getting your customers or clients out of deep doo-doo should they find themselves in it.

If someone gets arrested and put in jail, a lawyer will know what to do. So will a plumber if a pipe bursts during freezing weather. So will a vet if a client's pet gets injured.

But what about more subtle emergencies?

Here's where some well-placed advice in your blog posts can save your customers/clients from smaller disasters and make them thank their lucky stars that they gave you their business, especially as these small disasters are likely to happen when it's not possible for you to step in right away.

It will also intrigue and attract new customers/clients who may well not have seen such useful advice on your competitors' blogsites.

So, let's have a look at some examples…

Hairdressing business
- What to do if a home hair product irritates your scalp
- How to cope when you haven't got time to wash your hair
- What to do if your hair frizzes up in damp weather
- How to put your hair up quickly for a sudden date
- What to do if you experience sudden hair loss

Recording studio
- What to do if a recording you need has become corrupted somehow
- Basics on how to hook up your recording to a playback system
- What to do if one of your musicians doesn't make it to a session and you can't reschedule or afford another one
- Band politics: how to sort out creative arguments
- How to pick an emergency musician to sit in on a session

Jewellery dealer
- How to carry out emergency repairs to costume jewellery
- How to know if a stone is loose in a mounting
- How to guard against bracelet catches breaking
- How to make sure "butterfly" earring backs stay put
- What to do if a favourite ring is too big and might fall off

Fitness coach

- How to handle sudden muscular pain
- How to sooth stiff, sore muscles
- What to eat and drink if you've overdone a workout
- How to cope if you feel faint while working out
- How to tell if you're dehydrated

Figuring out some good "emergency" blog posts isn't difficult. It's merely a matter of thinking of the problems your customers or clients (and prospective customers/clients) might encounter, and putting yourself in their shoes ... how would you feel? And what advice would you feel is helpful right at that time?

REVIEWS

Don't yawn – reviews are useful if not to you, to your readers / customers.

The trouble with so many reviews in blog posts and website articles, however, is that they are written by the wrong person and are inappropriate for the audience concerned.

In other words, they are written by an expert who describes and judges the product or service as someone who has advanced knowledge of it.

Not, however, from the point of view of Mr or Ms A N Other who is likely to use the damned thing.

Customers may seem stupid, but their money and loyalty aren't

I can't count the number of product or service reviews I have read online about stuff that interests me, that leave me standing after the first sentence. I know I'm pretty stupid when it comes to techie stuff in particular, but it turns out I'm not alone.

Lots of people – customers and prospective customers – feel the same way that I do. We don't always get the finer points of product / service reviews.

This is purely because they have been written from a subjective point of view by people who don't appreciate that there are dimwits like me in cyberspace who buy such products and services nonetheless.

However we don't need or want to know the square root of the exponential giga-stonking factor that differentiates the product from its 347 competitors. We just want to know how it works plus whether or not it is better value than its competitors, and even more importantly, what it will do for us.

Ensure your reviews share your thoughts on your readers' terms

Whenever a new development crops up in your business area, use the opportunity to share your thoughts about new products and services.

Be sure to express that in terms that your readers / customers can understand, otherwise your opportunity for brand reinforcement will be lost.

Other people's reviews

I'm sure there always will be the temptation to lift reviews or relevant products and services and use those on your own blog.

Certainly, there's nothing wrong with using quotes from others' reviews as long as you attribute those to the right people.

But never forget that what your readers / customers expect, and what you have a duty to deliver, is your own take on whatever is the topic in question.

You know your readers / customers better than most, and they look to you to review products and services in the light of what's good for them.

Take that duty seriously … and be prepared to benefit as a result!

SERIES

Ever since the first soap opera, "Painted Dreams," was aired on a Chicago radio station back in 1930, serials and series have been used to hook listeners and viewers into a long running chain of communications.

The techniques work for the written word, too – especially for your business blog.

In the broadcast world, a **serial** (like a soap opera or shows like Dallas, Coronation Street, Eastenders, etc.) consists of XX programs each of which tell the next part of one long story. A **series** is XX programs using the same characters, sets, etc., in which each episode tells an entire standalone story (e.g. Silent Witness, New Tricks, Murder She Wrote, etc.)

These formats work for business blogs, too

Just like the soap operas, interesting, gripping series of blog posts can keep readers and customers coming back regularly to read your next instalment.

There are other advantages, too. Once a series is complete, you can package all "episodes" together, edit them appropriately and perhaps add some additional content and voilà – an instant eBook, and even a full size book for print and Kindle. See the Blog posts as a book section for more on how to compile blog posts into a book.

One good example of that is Lucy McCarraher's excellent series on HTWB, called "**How To Write Fiction Without The Fuss,**" which she has now turned into a very successful print and Kindle book.

How to format your series: A to Z

There are a number of ways in which you can format your series. Let's start with this one I've used a number of times: an A to Z.

Provided that your subject matter is pretty wide-reaching, you should be able to find 26 words that suggest topics each starting with the next letter of the alphabet, although Q, X and Z can be tricky.

Assuming that each article in your A to Z series runs to at least 500 words or so, you will end up with 13,000 words worth of information – more than enough to compile and edit into an eBook which you can then sell or give away as a promotional piece.

How to format your series: chronologically

Lucy's series, "**How To Write Fiction Without The Fuss,**" consisted of 26 articles that started at the beginning of the fiction writing journey and with each new "episode" stepped you through the process until by the end you have a good, finished manuscript.

The chronological series is ideal for any specific process that has a beginning, middle, and end – e.g., how to create a brand new beautiful garden out of the muddy, rubble-filled back yard of a newly built home … how to make curtains from start to finish … how to review, analyze, adjust and improve your financial investments … countdown to your house move … and so-on.

How to format your series: associated topics

This is a bit like the A to Z format without the need to find words corresponding to the next letter in the alphabet!

Subjects you might approach in this way are things like … tips to help you (achieve/do a variety of things within your topic) … guide to great restaurants in (area) … what you need to get ready for your accountant at tax return time … etc.

It's a useful way to assemble a group of related but relatively random topics under a series heading which, like all series, will help ensure your readers keep coming back to your blogsite for more information.

SHARING POSTS ON SOCIAL MEDIA

Further to what I've already mentioned in the Promoting Your Blog Posts section, when you share an article on your SocMed platforms it's only polite to give readers a taste of what's in it for them if they read it.

But recently I have been lambasted by two good cybercitizens – one in the UK and one in the USA – for not describing in detail the benefits of reading whatever article, chapter and verse, in sufficient detail, when I share either one of my own articles or someone else's.

By one I was told … "Try to be creative with it then. Think of the post as an extension of the link. Try to bring up something interesting to yourself, quote the post, describe the post in more detail, bring up further discussion based on the post... something, anything..."

Not everyone has time for creative musings on information online

Many people want to cut the crap and get straight to the point with social media and blogging. Long-winded preambles may please those who want to wallow in the bubble bath of what social media should be all about in an ideal world. But few business people now have the time or inclination to muse – they want news.

I can understand where these people are coming from, especially when you consider how much garbage is "shared" in the SocMed by robots and other mechanical means purely distributing links like confetti at a wedding.

But there's a big difference between giving a concise reason why something is worth reading ... and waffling on at length about a post that you feel someone would benefit from and trying to explain the whole post in your preamble.

What's the ideal style of preamble to a recommended blog post or similar?

Short, sharp and to the point. I've found that time and time again whether I'm sharing my own posts or someone else's.

You do NOT need to wax lyrical about the post: the fact that you're recommending it should be enough to tell your readers and followers that they would do well to check the article out.

Let's get real here, as I've mentioned. If you have something to share, great – so get on with it. Don't bore people with your own interpretation unless you feel that's as valuable as the post you're promoting, whether it's one of yours or someone else's.

If it is your own post, treat it as if it were someone else's

That allows you to use the third person and it will be more convincing.

Try to encapsulate not just what the post's about, but also what it will do for you-the-reader … but without making your words sound like advertising copy.

Some hypothetical examples

- Why (Poster) thinks she could reduce your book-keeping costs
- Think you know how to write convincingly? (Poster) thinks otherwise, and could be right.
- A pretty good summary of how you can upgrade your (whatever) which could save you time
- If you suffer from (whatever problem) you might find this advice helpful
- Not sure I agree with this post, but it certainly seems to save some (product) users a lot of time
- …and so-on.

Some examples of how to share blog posts

You need to be original to capture readers' imagination, whether sharing your own blog posts or someone else's.

Twitter

In the case of Twitter where realistically the limit is 120 characters max, often it's better not to use the title, but instead write a "teaser" line that's more personal and less direct than a title can be.

For example … my own article **"Restaurant jargon: gastronomic terms demystified"** got a respectable number of visits from Twitter when I tweeted the title with the link. But when I tweeted **"You'll never be able to read a menu and keep a straight face again"** the visits shot up by about 40 percent.

Sometimes there's only **room on Twitter for you to insert a couple of words.** But even that can spark extra interest in the tweet, among your followers. For example (my comments in caps)…

- BBC News - Sweden: Wedding ring 'found on carrot' after 16 years // **24 CARROT GOLD?**
- Brains of rats connected allowing them to share information via internet // **AH, SO WE HAVE THE RATNET NOW**
- Edinburgh Zoo Pandas Listen To Marvin Gaye's Mood Music Before Hanky Panky // **MARVIN GAYE? MEH**
- BBC News - 'Oldest marathon man' Fauja Singh runs last 10km race // **WONDERFUL MAN!**
- How to make a money vision board! // **GREAT IDEA TO INSPIRE YOUR BUSINESS**

Pinterest

As you know, Pinterest is mainly about sharing images rather than getting people to link through and read something. I get much more traffic from Pinterest now that I write a short descriptive piece of the article concerned and make it clear what I want readers to do next, rather than just look at the picture.

For example... this is the pin I wrote for the restaurant jargon article ...

Restaurant jargon: gastronomic terms demystified, part 1 ... *I love eating out – don't you? But so often we can be disappointed by the realities emerging from the yummy-sounding jargon on the menus. Here is part one of my, er, interpretations of those terms. Please add your thoughts to these ....!*

The cover of my book "How To Smile Through Cancer," with these words to describe it and make it clear that it's a new book, not a picture:

How To Smile Through Cancer ... Despite many cancers now becoming much more survivable, in itself it is not funny. What can be funny, though, are the often hilarious things that can happen when dealing with doctors, nurses, hospitals, chemo-baldness, prostheses, ultra-sound tests, examinations and loads more ancillary issues which invariably you trip over while going through your cancer journey. That's what this book is all about...

And another article which got a lot of traffic from Pinterest: "OK, hands up! Who stole SOCIAL?"

OK. Hands up! Who stole SOCIAL? ... If you're fond of writing, there's nothing more irritating than a bunch of knobhead technofreaks coming along and snatching a perfectly respectable word to use for their own nefarious purposes ... read on for some laughs with humourist and business writer Suzan St Maur from HowToWriteBetter.net

Do the same for your shares of other people's articles, posts, tweets, etc. and help increase their traffic too

About an article in the Harvard Business Review, based on "Don't anesthetize your colleagues with bad writing..."

*This is an interesting follow-up of an article (not one of mine, sadly!) called "**Don't anesthetize your colleagues with bad writing**" that appeared in the Harvard Business Review a while ago - there's a link to the original article further down on this page FYI...*

About an article written by a colleague whose opinions I respect very much: "How to fix three common online marketing mistakes" ...
Good article by my friend and client Ann Handley from the US site MarketingProfs.com. Do you agree with what she says about social media?

About another article, "Writing with personality for a business blog"...

Really excellent blog post by a friend of my son's, who has graduated from Uni and got a job in Social Media, God help him... ;-)

About a case study of employees with disabilities, "Best practice case studies, the National Trust"

*The National Trust run a course called **Passport to Your Future**, the aim of which is to encourage people from a diverse range of backgrounds to think about working in the Heritage sector. This is the story of one young man who benefited hugely from the scheme...*

And so-on. It's not difficult; it merely takes a little longer to add a sentence or two to explain why you like the post or article, and why others should like it.

It's almost a courtesy; and it shows that the share has been done by a live human, not a software robot. It really does increase traffic, too.

SOCIAL MEDIA AS A BLOG POST SOURCE

If you're scratching around looking for blog topics to write about in your business, professional or industry area, you might find just the thought triggers you need in the social media groups, communities and circles you frequent.

According to my good friend, professional cohort and recently published star author Jon Baker, observing and participating in your relevant groups on platforms like LinkedIn can be an absolute goldmine of suggestions for blog posts for you. And I agree.

So how do you access these business blog topic leads?

Simple: by joining the right groups and communities. But just joining and having the occasional scroll through them isn't enough.

What's important is that you participate in those groups. Read the posts and comments. Comment yourself (in itself, an excellent way to promote yourself and your blog for expertise and advice in your subject area.)

Chiefly, the groups you need to look at for business blogging, you'll find on LinkedIn, Google Plus, and to a lesser extent on Facebook. I know there are other platforms out there too and of course I don't exclude them – but these three, for the moment, seem to be where business conversations are happening most.

But it's not just about the platforms. Where you will find the best options for yourself and your business is in the business groups (or in the case of Google Plus, their communities.)

What groups should you seek for business blog post inspiration?

Here are my own ideas of the type of groups or communities that would be helpful for you...

Your own industry. An obvious choice, but be careful, because this category is likely to be populated with many of your competitors and you might find yourself fighting it out with a number of others over certain points in discussions. If you're happy with that, fine – go for it.

Allied industries and business areas. Let's say you're a yoga teacher. Not only will you find interesting discussions in groups and communities concerned with yoga, but also you might benefit from engaging in discussions in groups connected with health, fitness, dieting, exercise and other similar topics. Here, general fitness etc. question and issues raised might provide you with just the opportunity you need to answer with advice on how your yoga teaching could help, and of course provide you with an idea for a blog post about that on your site.

Local business groups. Particularly on LinkedIn and to a lesser extent on Google Plus and Facebook, local business groups and communities are very strong. In these cases you have the added advantage of providing not only your expertise, but your expertise available within geographically, F-2-F reach. Particularly if you are a yoga teacher or in another business providing offline products and services, such groups – despite being online – are very valuable.

What about inspiration for business blog topics in a more general sense?

Once again depending on the nature of your business, it can be well worthwhile to keep your finger on the pulse of not only your own industry, but those of **allied industries** as well, right across the whole internet – social media included.

Obviously you will glean a lot through your participation in business groups as described above, but also you will learn more by keeping an ear to the ground in more general terms.

For that purpose, as I've mentioned earlier, I strongly recommend **Google Alerts** – a service which for now at least is free, and is absolutely priceless in the way it can keep you up to speed on what's happening in almost any sphere you're interested in. Simply type in the keywords you want and it will keep you informed of everything that's going on within the internet on the topic concerned. Brilliant.

SWEARING

Are you guilty of using a foul word or two in your blogposts, emails, comments, Facebook/Twitter posts *et al*? Do you think they enhance what you've written – or do they make you look foul-mouthed?

I know I am guilty of using words that I shouldn't. Many of my articles, posts, comments etc. are peppered with (usually mild) profanities which tend to roll off the virtual tongue quite easily – or at least they do if you are, as I am, surrounded by lippy young people who fire off swear words if they so much as misplace a sandwich or find a hair extension out of place.

As such, the use of disgraceful language does have a nasty habit of becoming second nature. And I know that's no excuse...

There are many people out there – and not just older folks – who find swearing objectionable, and you can't blame them. Mostly they have been brought up to believe that swearing and cursing are disrespectful to the majority of people.

My parents and others of their generation put across, to me, the diktat that the use of swear words merely demonstrated one's ignorance and lack of vocabulary (mind you, that all went out of the window when one of them stepped on a live wasp or slammed their finger in a car door.)

Two categories – religious, and vulgar

As far as I can see it, swearwords in our modern age fall into two categories:

- Religious cursing
- Vulgarisms

Religious cursing is very sensitive for many people and it's something I try to avoid – don't you? But what about words like "damn," damned," or "damning?" Despite those appearing largely innocuous these days, should someone wish to take it to the limit, there could be a religious connotation here.

And that doesn't even begin to infiltrate what some people write using terms that may offend a whole host of religions from Christian to Judaism to Islam to who knows how many more. So is it appropriate to use religiously orientated swear words in our writing? In my humble opinion, **absolutely no way**.

OK, how about the serious vulgarisms?

Here's where we enter relatively uncharted waters. I remember once asking my father where he thought the word **f*ck** came from, and he – as a veteran of WW2 – trotted out the explanation that it's an acronym standing for "For Unlawful Carnal Knowledge." Nice one. But is it true?

According to Wikipedia, the origins of the F-word are vague... so I doubt that my Pop's answer was correct, convenient though it may have seemed at the time. Snopes.com seems to agree with me on that one.

And then there is the ultimate vulgarism (or at least so most of us think) – **c*nt**. Where does this awful, horrible word come from?

Wikipedia, bless them, have explored this one to a helpful extent and say, "the earliest citation of this usage in the 1972 Oxford English Dictionary, c 1230, **refers to the London street known as Gropecunt Lane.** Scholar Germaine Greer has said that "it is one of the few remaining words in the English language with a genuine power to shock."

Especially if one were to have the misfortune to walk down Gropecunt Lane, I'm sure, although according to Wikipedia (http://en.wikipedia.org/wiki/Gropecunt_Lane) this was quite a commonly used road name in medieval times in England and was ascribed to roads frequented by prostitutes. Nothing like calling a spade a spade, huh.

Maybe it's the connotation, but maybe, too, it's the sound of the word. Germaine was right. Would you use this word in any of your writing? OK, but there are lesser swearwords that express our thoughts so well, and they don't resonate with quite the same impact.

Does swearing actually have a legitimate place in our writing?

This is where it gets a bit more interesting. Swearing, whether the purists like it or not, is a very common element in our every-day parlance. It's part of our modern culture.

So, do we – as people charged with reflecting realistically this modern culture in our writing – pronounce judgment and exclude swearing as naughty, smutty, dirty and undesirable? Should we adopt the nanny-like stance of television drama in which even evil villains, murderers, drug dealers, etc. only say a mere "bloody" here and a "sh*t" there?

Or should we incorporate the swearing that people use in everyday speech, into the writing we do in our blogs, comments, posts, articles and more?

When in doubt, leave it out

Given that swearwords are such a sensitive issue, it does makes sense to leave them out unless you're absolutely certain that your readers will take them in the way you have intended.

Tip? Use your common sense!

TESTIMONIALS

Testimonials have a bit of a dubious history. It's only in comparatively recent times, when advertising in most industrialized countries has been regulated, that readers know testimonials have to be genuine - or else. There may still be the odd person or two who sneers at testimonials and endorsements, but in the main people now accept them for real, and believe in their honesty. This makes them powerful.

However getting a good testimonial isn't easy, and for a variety of reasons must not be "written" by someone other than the person giving it. Without putting words in someone's mouth, then, how do you go about getting good testimonials for your blog, as well as for your business, website, CV/résumé, etc?

Use a positive, journalistic interview technique

If you simply ask someone to give you a testimonial without giving them any guidelines, you're leaving it up to luck as to the quality and nature of their response. It's far more effective to interview the person, whether face-to-face or my email, because by using specifically designed questions you can draw out the points you need to feature.

For more about how to get a good interview, see the Interviews section.

Who does the interview?

If you're working on a face-to-face basis, you are the wrong person to conduct the interview. That's because your client or customer may feel a little intimidated if you are the person s/he has actually acquired the product or service from. You need to use a neutral third party who will not intimidate the interviewee in the same way, and can probably get away with asking more pointed questions than you can.

With email, though, because it's a step removed from direct personal contact, you can write your questions yourself. I find the way that gets the best responses in email interviews is to list the questions with spaces between them and ask the interviewee to hit "reply" and then write their answers under each question.

The basic needs

What you need to focus on whichever approach you use, is how you/your company:

- Solved their problems
- Saved them money
- Made their business more efficient
- Improved employee morale
- Enabled greater productivity
- Improved service to their customers
- Increased their sales

- Helped them get ahead of their competitors
- Got them the winning tender
- Made their patients better
- Improved their sex appeal
- and so-on.

The essential questions to ask

We can begin by taking a leaf out of a journalist's book, and never ask a question that can be answered with a "yes" or a "no." The easiest way to do that is to start all questions with, once again, the journalist's old favourites of "who, what, why, how, when and where."

Questions that lead to good testimonial responses:

- What is it that you think makes XXX different from their competitors?
- Earlier on, you mentioned that XXX is better than their competitors. Why would you say that is?
- Just how much better than the competition do you feel XXX really is?
- Why do you feel that XXX is more efficient than other, similar (whatever)?
- How would you rate your experience of working with/using XXX?
- Compared with their competitors, how would you rate your experience of working with/using XXX?

- On a 1 to 10 scale, how would you rate your experience of working with/using XXX, and why?
- What difference has using XXX made to your business's/department's performance?
- What is it about XXX's performance/service that makes the different?
- What was it that made you choose XXX in the first place?
- What was it that made you choose XXX instead of their competitors?
- What was it that made you change from your previous (whatever) to XXX?
- What additional benefits have you found through using XXX?
- Of all the benefits of XXX we've talked about, which is the most important to you, and why?
- What are the three main benefits of working with XXX?
- In summary, then, what would you say is the key benefit of working with XXX?
- In summary, then, what difference has working with/using XXX made to your bottom line?
- How important is it to you that you should work with/use XXX in the future?
- What sort of future do you think XXX can look forward to?
- If I were someone considering using XXX, what advice would you give me?

How many questions?

Fewer rather than more, if possible, although it's sometimes worth putting an important question in again during the interview or in the email, obviously phrased differently, so you get two opportunities to get a good answer. In an email interview I seldom use more than 6 or 7 questions … people have a low boredom threshold with email and in any case are usually pushed for time.

What happens next

Once your interview is done, it's time to edit the quotes you want to use. If you have done a face-to-face interview and audio recorded it, get it transcribed; it's much easier to edit on paper/screen than whizzing back and forth on a sound track. If your ultimate need is for audio quotes, you'll find them very easily on the sound track from the edited written notes.

Always use real quotes without making up bits to compensate for shortcomings, and don't polish them up. The occasional grammatical mistake or bit of harmless slang makes it much more realistic.
Then always, always run the finished testimonial past whoever has said it, for their approval. Often people will tell you not to bother but I feel that it's a courtesy you should not ignore.

The other point you need to clarify with the testimonial giver is how they want to be acknowledged.

Some will want to retain their anonymity but if you are to be believed, you must ask them to agree to substantiate their quote privately if someone were to challenge it. Very few people will refuse to do that.

Others will want some sort of credit; for example, their website's URL. If so, that's great!

THREATS YOUR READERS FACE, AS BLOG TOPICS

You don't want to be a scare mongerer, but it does make sense for you to warn your readers / customers about things you can envisage as potential threats – and how they can prepare for them and deal with them if and when they arise.

Obviously you can't suddenly leap into their businesses and swashbuckle away threats that aren't within your remit. However within that remit of yours, potentially there is quite a lot that you can contribute which will reassure your customers and prospects that you are (or can be) in there looking after their best interests.

OK – how about some examples?

Your business is: a dental practice

Well, there are no surprises about what threats your clients and prospects could find out here! However – especially but not exclusively – if you run an entirely private (i.e. not government funded) practice dental practice, scare mongering might just work out to be a no-no.

I went to a private dentist once to have my jacket crowns checked and was told, after x-rays, that the "pegs" on which my current crowns were hung were utterly rotten and likely to drop my entire dental array into the next plate of pasta I would eat, sure as hell.

I smelled a rat, so went to another dentist whom I trust – a dentist who works within the UK's NHS - and who, after x-raying, said ... well, I won't share what she said because it was extremely rude and contained several 4-letter words.

But you get the picture.

My "pegs" were fine. That private dentist was a charlatan.

Moral to this story? Although you may want to scare your clients and prospects into getting their teeth checked more regularly, don't overdo it. And apart from telling them they need to check in with you regularly, be sure to help them look after their teeth and gums effectively at home.

Your business: an electrical contractor

Once again, no surprises for blog post ideas: if your electrics are old / worn out / inappropriate you could be asking for a fire in your home. Endless options for warning blog posts here, especially in European countries where we seem to waft over modernization of such things and "make do" with old sh*t that we shouldn't.

How to be sure you're prepared for an electricity outage – candles, matches, torches/flashlights, oil lamps, etc. ... what to do about switching off appliances etc in an outage ... who to contact (in your local area) to find out news on an outage... etc.

Safety with household appliances, power points, extension leads, etc. ... particularly safety with children and power points and appliances...

Your business: travel agency

This might appear to be a bit of a no-no where you're concerned because the last thing you want your clients to think is that there could be problems attached to your service! However, you can turn that particular issue around to your advantage.

For starters, you can blog about the dangers of using untried resources on the internet for booking travel and holidays ... the downsides of the "last minute" booking options ... "

Then, depending on the nature of your particular business you can examine the pros and cons of booking "direct" to owners of holiday properties as against booking such things via an agency (like yours) which checks such properties out and eliminates the bad ones...

And so-on.

Use your imagination to consider the threats your readers may be facing

As one of their key suppliers, you will know (or should know) what their businesses could be facing, so address those in some of your blog posts. Doing that will almost certainly gain you kudos.

And if you want to pursue this one further, in a blog post ask your readers to share what their key threats are.

Responses can form the basis of very interesting and very relevant blog posts leading to good discussions not only on your site, but as conversations across your areas of social media.

By sharing the upshot of all this you could well be doing your readers (and customers) a substantial favour, and doing yourself a substantial favour, too.

TIPS, COUNTDOWNS AND CHECKLISTS AS BLOG POSTS

All the so-called blogging experts out there will swear up and down that posts headed "Top Ten Tips to (whatever result)" are a sure-fire way of attracting lots of traffic to your site. I'm a little worried that the "tips" format has become just too much of a cliché, and that readers seeing such a headline will yawn and move on to something a bit fresher – on another site. But that's just me being picky.

Tips

Certainly, tips have the advantage of providing you with a vehicle for a collection of short pieces of advice on a topic that you can then display in no particular order.

If you're going to use that format, make sure that you adjust the number of tips according to the amount you want to say, so that your overall word count is under 1,000. Readers' attention spans are getting shorter all the time which means there's increasing pressure on bloggers to keep it short, tight and sweet.

So with tips, if – say - each tip takes 100 words to explain, you don't want to include more than 10 tips in the whole piece. If your tips are much shorter though – say 20 words each – you can up the overall number of tips, although you still don't want to take that to the limit and include 50 tips.

The trouble with as many as 50 is, no matter how short they are the concept of 50 tips will make readers think they haven't got time to read them all… even though that's erroneous.

Checklists

Checklists are useful for a series of actions or points you want readers to consider in related order, but are not necessarily directly related to each other. Some examples…

Car dealer – checklist of things to check on your car before winter

Wedding planner – checklist of crucial stages of the wedding planning process

Horse riding trainer – checklist of all the things you need to pack into your vehicle before going to a horse show

Countdowns

These are seen less frequently but are a very good and useful way to help your readers tackle a series of actions or points in a given sequence. For example...

Car dealer – countdown to starting your car on frosty morning

Wedding planner – countdown to the wedding day

Horse riding trainer – your horse's warm-up countdown to a dressage test

Topics

Tips, checklists and countdowns are very handy ways to repurpose earlier content. If you look back through some of your earlier articles you'll probably spot quite a few that could be turned into one of these lists.

Similarly, when you write a full article on a given topic, you may well find that you can develop a list from it at the same time. Then you can do one of three things:

1. Incorporate the list into the article
2. Run the list as your next blog post, as a follow-up
3. Run the list some months later, as a reminder

All you need to is add a short introduction and summary, and voilà — ready-made blog post that won't take you long to put together but that will be useful and interesting for your readers.

UNSAFE FOR WORK

"Unsafe for work" is a bit of a cheat really as the proper term is "not safe for work," but as it's an important issue to think about with your business blogging I hope you'll forgive the small transgression.

Obviously we're not looking at many people who are going to blog about porn and other lewd topics in their business blog posts, but the issue goes beyond the obvious and can even include the use of relatively mild swearwords.

Here's what Wikipedia has to say about it:

Not suitable/safe for work (NSFW) is Internet slang or shorthand. Typically, the NSFW tag is used in e-mail, videos, and on interactive discussion areas (such as Internet forums, blogs, or community websites) to mark URLs or hyperlinks which contain material such as nudity, violence, pornography or profanity, which the viewer may not want to be seen accessing in a public or formal setting such as at work.

Unsurprisingly the term has given rise to numerous bawdy-laughter parodies and even a TV series using that name. Provided you're pretty broad-minded and have a good sense of humour, a lot of it is very funny. But not everyone feels that way - especially a) in a business context and even more importantly b) in your customers' opinions.

So how do you benchmark what is and isn't safe for work?

Unfortunately however many people you ask, you'll get a slightly different answer each time as to where you draw the line. Everyone does draw a line somewhere but it can be anywhere from hardcore pornography to using words like "damn" and "blast."

As I have mentioned earlier in this book, **StumbleUpon, that delightfully virtuous sharing platform so popular in the USA especially,** once told me to go sit on the naughty step and I was not allowed to share any more that day. Not having used any four-letter words or anything vaguely sexy in my text I was puzzled when suddenly I realized that I had used the word "whiskey." I removed the word and hey presto, I was teacher's pet again.

Quite why children would be reading business blog posts and becoming instant alcoholics as a result of that one, I'm not sure. Frankly most 9-year-olds know more about booze, designer drugs and sex than I do and would regard whiskey to be about as appealing as knitting lessons with grandma. But StumbleUpon obviously disagrees and that can't have been a frivolous decision.

Here are some suggestions of key areas to avoid:

- Racism
- Sexism
- Ageism
- Homophobia
- Explicit things about sex
- Rude words and harsh vulgarisms
- Offensive remarks about religion, and religious swearwords
- Vulgar/offensive comments about minority groups, people with disabilities, etc.
- ...plus anything else that your common sense tells you.

What you also need to watch out for depending on your audience

- Reference to alcohol and drugs
- Darwin and evolution (if your audience is mainly Christian, especially in southern USA)
- Anything connected with sex
- Gay marriage
- Political views
- ...plus anything else that knowledge of your readers tells you.

That's the key, as always: know your readers and that knowledge will guide you to write what works well for them.

UPDATING OLDER BLOG POSTS

Should you update older posts on your blog, and if so how should you do it? Most bloggers feel it's right to do this. The whys and wherefores of how to do it are a little less clear. But it's not usually enough to expect readers to check a blog post's publication date so they realize it was accurate only when it was published.

Regular updating has a number of advantages, so read on...

Here are my recommendations on how to do it, but this advice is by no means conclusive.

That's because blog posts in various industrial topics will have equally varying sell-by dates and hence, varying requirements for updating in a particular way.

Does your blog need to be updated according to laws or other legislation?

If the answer is yes, it's a no brainer.

You must keep it up to date or not only will your readers find it odd that you should be lagging behind the times, but also you might even get a rap on the knuckles from officialdom for putting forward outdated information.

Watch your information very carefully.

What about technological updating?

This is not something you necessarily need to watch out for due to legal reasons, but it's certainly something you need to consider for professional reasons if your blog is to remain at the forefront of your technological audience.

No matter how busy you might get with your techie stuff, never forget that your blog is probably your key marketing tool.

So update the techie stuff as often as you can.

And at the same time, update the human interpretations of your techie stuff on an equally frequent basis (assuming your decision-making paying customers are not techies) so everyone knows just how good and up-to-date you are.

How to go about updating your older posts

The most obvious way is to go into the older post and make the necessary changes, hit "update," and you're done. But is this the best and most honest way to do it? Or should you make it obvious that you have revisited and updated the post, so making your readers realize that you have made the update after the original post was published?

Personally, I prefer to do one of the following things:

Insert a "stop press." Insert a new paragraph about the item concerned and either indent it, or highlight it as a pull quote, and head it something like "Stop Press: new rules as at (date here)" ... or perhaps just "Update on technical spec as at (date here)."

Although you can install a "redirect" element within an old post to show readers where to go to find out the most up to date information, this is not necessarily the ideal solution. Whether to use a redirect or a **"stop press"** approach depends quite a lot, I would say, on how much of the original post is out of date. If it's just one issue, it's probably worth using a "stop press" update and then re-promoting the original post. However if there are two or more points that need updating, you'd be better off using a redirect to an entirely new post.

Include your updates as comments on your original post. This has the added advantage of inviting readers to engage in a new discussion about your original post.

Write a new post altogether. This is probably the best option for SEO purposes, as long as the majority of the text is new and fresh. However you can use substantial quotes from the original post, interspersing those with the new information.

VERBOSITY

I'm the last writer in the world to object to words, verbosity-laden or not. But even I have to admit that too many words suck. How can you write what you want to express in your business blog posts without overdoing the verbiage? Here are some thoughts.

Are your readers as keen on your topic as you are?

Much as I can appreciate how much you love your topic and want to write enthusiastically about it in your business blog writing, bear in mind that your readers probably don't share your enthusiasm to the same degree.

That doesn't mean that they don't care: of course they do. What it does mean, though, is that in your blog writing you need to condense your own views, opinions, recommendations and more, into text that gets the key points over to your readers without the verbosity that you perhaps might feel is necessary for you and other experts in your field.

Your readers don't necessarily want to know all the technical details

If your business is in any way complicated you are, understandably, likely to want to share with your customers your explanations of various processes and other detailed activities.

There's a useful way to handle this bulk of ancillary information: section it off into a separate area of your website or blogsite, and link to that. This way your readers/customers know where to find the full story if they want to read it, but in the meantime are not going to be bogged down by verbosity when otherwise they could be reading more about the big picture.

Unless you operate in a particularly technical business area, chances are your customers will be a lot more interested in what your product or service can do for their management / IT efficiency / overall bottom line than they are in verbosity.

Never forget that what your customers want to read about is not what your product or service is - it's what your product or service will do for them, and how it will make them feel.

What about sheer over-writing?

We've all heard the story about someone - ranging from Mark Twain to Abraham Lincoln to who-knows-who - saying something like "I'm sorry I didn't have time to write you a short note, so here is a long one."

Writing concisely is a lot harder than writing at length. We business blog writers all know that. But how - and by how much - should we really cut down on our verbosity-ridden text?

Although other business blog writing experts do advocate very harsh editing, I'm not quite so violent by nature. It's all very well to prune your text hard: but there's a big difference between that and pruning it so hard it loses all its personality.

If you want your text to be punchy by all means be strict with your editing, but don't take out all your little personal quirks and eccentricities that make your text absolutely yours. To a large extent that's what differentiates it from everyone else's text in your marketplace.

VIDEO

As technology moves us farther and farther on in terms of what we can achieve with relatively simple kit to put ourselves online in visual and audio terms as well as in pure text, we can be grateful that decent quality video has finally become affordable for nearly everyone.

With video cameras being so easy to use and video material being so easy to upload, it's not surprising that many people think it's equally easy to produce good video content and performance.

Even with good quality Smartphones, it's now possible to produce a high-end video that previously only would have been possible to achieve with far more elaborate equipment.

So now, the production quality of video is no longer a problem. What is still a problem, is the way people think they can shoot it, edit it, and upload it to their blogs and hey presto – a video that will impress the hell out of your clients/customer, prospects, employees, colleagues and more.

However, they're wrong.

No matter how simple it has become to shoot, edit and produce a reasonable quality video to use on your blog at a DIY level, if you get the content wrong it will still make you look amateurish and foolish.

No amount of technology can improve on a bad performance.

The camera exaggerates even the slightest movement and makes it look maniacal. On the other hand, once you recognize this point and make yourself sit absolutely bolt still, you'll look like a ventriloquist's dummy. It takes a lot of training and practice to hit the right balance, as any TV newsreader will tell you.

Interviews

The answer? Unless you happen to be very good at on-camera presenting, don't do it. Instead use the **off-camera interview technique.**

This technique is often used on TV by news reporters and documentary directors, where you see the interviewee talking to an unseen someone just beside the camera.

It's brilliant for two reasons: one, the camera in this case is recording one half of a genuine conversation between two people which is far more natural and relaxed than a "talking head" and two, you don't have to remember your lines in anything like the same detail.

All it needs is for someone to sit beside the camera (or it can be the person running the camera, depending on whether you use remote control or not) and ask questions to the interviewee - which you will have pre-agreed, but not over-rehearsed.

You, as interviewer, then look at the person (so your eye line ends just to one side of the camera) and listen to their reply. Your questions can then be cut out afterwards, or if you really like the "fly-on-the-wall" approach, you can leave them in.

Whoever asks the questions, you/they must take care not to phrase them in such a way that you automatically respond with either a "yes" or a "no" as this can make the dialogue fall rather flat. The way to avoid that is to ask "open" questions and these are what journalists use – start every question with:

- what
- who
- where
- why
- when
- which
- how
- etc.

And finally, leave a short gap between the question and your answer so that if you decide to edit out the questions later, it can be done cleanly. Similarly, don't talk over each other as that can mess up the soundtrack.

Another damning element of some amateur videos can be that **the voice of the speaker sounds like s/he was talking from the bottom of a well** – echoing, hollow and distorted.

This usually arises when you are using the camera microphone to record the sound; no matter how much camera manufacturers swear up and down that their on-camera mics are of excellent quality, in the main they are not.

Rather than go to the expense and palaver of setting up individual mics, you can simply ensure that the place where you record your video is as sound-dead as possible. A nice, fluffy, thickly carpeted, softly furnished living room is ideal, well away from domestic noises. And avoid shooting in large open spaces, outdoors, and anywhere with hard floors and few soft furnishings.

For more information on conducting interviews

See the Interviews chapter,, and/or read the tutorials on HTWB, as mentioned above:

http://howtowritebetter.net/tutorial-how-to-interview-like-a-pro-business-journalist-part-1/

http://howtowritebetter.net/tutorial-how-to-interview-like-a-pro-business-journalist-part-2/

WRITING STYLE

Many so-called blogging experts write exhaustively on how important it is to be yourself, natural, relaxed and everyday in the writing style for your business blog. When you meet some of them face to face you soon realize that their blogging style is vastly different from how they speak in real life.

Much as I agree that your writing style in your blogging must be as close as possible to what and who you really are, it's nonsense to say that you should write exactly as you speak. F-2-F conversation is littered with "ums," "ahs," grunts and other things you wouldn't want to include in your written work.

More important, though, is that a live conversation tends to go around in circles, up hills, down valleys and off at tangents which, if you were to transcribe it verbatim, would make no sense at all.

So how do we get a writing style that's "as people speak?"

Basically, we take the way you speak as our raw material, and then give it structure so it can appear as coherent text. Here is an adapted excerpt from one of my earlier books, "Business Writing Made Easy," which suggests how you can do this...

To write as people speak instantly knocks down barriers and makes your message seem friendlier, more plausible, and so more attractive. The internet has done a wonderful job of championing this style of writing and has made it pretty well mandatory. And of course its influence has been championed to a huge extent in blogging.

Ah, easy though it sounds, achieving that fluency and simplicity of style isn't the piece of cake it appears to be. If for no other reason, most of us have had the "formal" brand of English brainwashed into our minds from schooldays and that's a hard one to eradicate.

So what's the answer?

Talk, don't write

When you're writing a blog post, forget the fact that you have to commit words to paper or screen. Instead imagine you're talking to a typical member of your audience.

You'll be amazed at how much easier the writing process becomes when you do this. That's because most of us are much more familiar with "talk" mode than we are with "write" mode, so in "talk" mode our thoughts flow more easily.

However, basic conversation tends to ramble. So it makes sense to plan your "talk" around a structure of short bullet points, so you don't stray.

Then "talk" away. Ideally, record it, transcribe it, then edit and tidy it up - and restructure it if necessary. If you can't physically record it then imagine yourself talking through and write down those words, followed by re-structuring, editing and tidying.

It works. Even if you only have a few minutes to get the job done, it still works. And your business blog writing will be all the more effective for it.

Some hints on how to sharpen up your writing style a bit

As I mentioned above, live conversation tends to be a bit messy, so it's a good idea to tidy it up by removing all unnecessary adjectives and adverbs, and replace vague or passive phrases with more direct, active voice.

Whatever you do, however, don't replace informal phrases with jargon or corporate-speak!

If you're writing a blog post that appears without an attribution to an individual - e.g. a company blog post - ensure that the writing style to be used is agreed with all who need to agree it, and fight tooth and nail to keep the business waffle and corporate bragging out of it.

When you're editing and tidying, don't get carried away. Over-editing is almost as bad as under-editing, because it strangles the personality out of the blog post and makes it come over as staccato and antiseptic. See the section on Editing.

XMAS, OTHER SPECIAL DAYS AND SEASONAL LINKS, AS BLOG POST THEMES

Making use of holidays and other special occasions as a way of creating topical blog posts is a good idea, provided that you use such occasions in an intelligent way that helps to promote your business ... and stands out from everyone else who might be trying to make a noise along similar lines.

Here are just a few dates that might inspire you come up with some good links with what you do. The following are based on what's celebrated in the UK where I live, but please apply this thinking to any other dates that are key in your own country/culture.

New Year. One of the biggest problems with New Year is that everyone crashes in on it and all you see on the internet for several days before and after is posts, advertising and all manner of other things saying "Happy New Year and here are the resolutions you should make" along with numerous variations on "Happy New Year and buy my stuff now." So, if you want to capitalise on the New Year you need to make sure your post - and especially your headline and structure - are very, very well focused on your readership and customers. Provided you do that, these are good.

Burn's Night. If you're Scottish or have any connections with Scotland - either via yourself or your products and services - Burn's Night on January 25th is an excellent opportunity to bring wistful tears to the eyes of Scots expats everywhere and row in your thoughts on Scotch whisky and other traditional Scottish exports. Surprisingly, haggis (the traditional Burn's supper meal served along with tatties and neeps) is becoming a celebrated fare elsewhere in the UK and I'm sure, in other parts of the world where people of Scottish descent live.

Valentine's Day. Whatever you sell or whatever service you offer, provided that it's reasonably within the B2C (Business To Consumer) range of interests you'll almost certainly find a hook to Valentine's Day on February 14th that will provide you with an opportunity to sell something - especially if you do special offers for Valentine's Day couples. Once again, as in New Year, you're up against squillions of other business bloggers offering Valentine's deals to their readers, so you need to make sure your offering is well targeted to your known readership/customer base.

St David's Day. March 1st - the celebration for Wales. In international terms St David's Day isn't likely to attract quite so much attention as the major landmarks do, so if you - and/or your customers and readers - have a connection with Wales this is the time to go for it. Daffodils and leeks are symbols connected with Wales, too, so should your business champion either of these this is also a useful time.

St Patrick's Day. March 17th - the Irish celebration. Given that there are people of Irish descent all over the world, this can be a wonderful opportunity to capitalise on either your Irish connections and/or Irish-related products and services. However be aware that Ireland has political issues with the UK, and despite the fact that most normal, intelligent people believe that mutual respect is essential, there are some people who disagree with that. If by any chance some of your customers are within those groups, be careful.

Easter. Another Christian festival which is celebrated quite widely and scatters brightly coloured eggs, bunnies, chicks, chocolates and various other fattening symbols across every imaginable portal. Once again, be warned that everyone else is going to be flaunting Easter bunnies in most B2C marketplaces so make sure your own offering is relevant if you want it to stand out. NB: Orthodox Easter tends to be a week or so later than the Anglican version, so check this out if your readers are predominantly within Orthodox cultures.

St George's Day. Yes, you heard ... England has a patron saint and his name is George. Amazingly St George's Day on April 23rd is not celebrated in England to anything like the extent of the saints connected to Scotland, Wales and Ireland, but protests against this lack of enthusiasm are growing and St George's Day is becoming more appreciated. If you're English and/or your products/services are English, cash in on the growing promotion of this jolly old saint and gear your business blog posts accordingly.

May Day. In a number of countries this is a public holiday (ostensibly May 1st but in many places the first Monday in May) and usually this is connected with the labour force. So if your product/service is connected with that, this is your chance to use it.

May 24th. A long weekend (around this date) in Canada during which many people buy and plant their gardens for the summer, knowing that further frost or snow is unlikely! As we Canadians have a fondness for history and tradition and stuff, this holiday has been celebrated for umpty-dump years as May 24th was the UK's late Queen Victoria's birthday. I know, I know. But if you're in Canada and have an interest either in Queen Victoria or gardening, this is the time to get blogging for business. NB: this is also **Memorial Day** in the USA, when veterans are celebrated for their sacrifices and honour.

Various public holidays during summer months. These vary from country to country but on a local basis they are likely to provide opportunities for businesses to blog about vacations, short breaks, activities for families, things for school children to do while on holiday, etc.

Back to school. Useful chances for businesses selling anything from child care to school clothing to get in on the frenzy. Timing is critical though: too early and customers won't want to think about "back to school" yet, and too late will see them having bought already from your competitors.

Halloween. A good time for blogging about your business if it involves jack- o-'lanterns, dressing up, costumes, candy/sweets, party favours, etc. Be careful if you're in the UK though: many people here object to the "trick or treat" concept and are very unwelcoming to goblins and spooks turning up on the doorstep asking for goodies.

Bonfire Night (UK). Thanks to a certain Mr Guy Fawkes who tried to blow up the London Parliament back in 1605, in the UK we celebrate his failure by blowing up thousands of fireworks which children enjoy and I loathe because the noise terrifies my dogs. Previously bonfires were lit to help the celebrations along but these are receding now as there have been so many accidents with them. Not an especially good business blogging opportunity unless you sell fireworks.

Thanksgiving. In October in Canada, late November in the USA. In the USA, at least, this is arguably the most important family get-together time of the year and for people blogging about anything to do with catering, food, recipes, turkeys, pumpkins, etc. it's potentially a busy time. Plus you get all the smashing sale offers that accompany those dates. See below.

Black Friday / Cyber Monday. A recently manufactured (by marketers, we assume) phenomenon, these days which occur immediately after the US Thanksgiving are being taken up in other countries now. Black Friday is a major shopping day often seen as the beginning of the Christmas/Holiday shopping season, so everyone is rushing to offer their customers the best bargains possible. Cyber Monday is its online equivalent, with a hefty push to get people to shop online for the Holidays and beyond.

Hannuka. A Jewish festival that's celebrated, or at least appreciated, by many. An obvious opportunity if your business involves Jewish-related products and/or services, but even if it doesn't - it's a time to share.

And, Christmas. A flurry of sales-orientated blogs in whatever business you're in. But unless you want your business blog posts to disappear into the flurry of Christmas hysteria, make sure your posts are focused on your readers and what they need - as always - and your Christmas wishes will be truly appreciated.

How about more subtle connections?

Instead of – or in addition to – the more usual seasonal topics and offers you can put together for your business blog, you can also use special dates around the calendar in a more metaphorical way … still topical, but not so closely related. For example… (please note I have mentioned just few religion-based holidays and occasions but as you well know there are hundreds more!)

Fall/autumn – back to school, harvest, falling leaves, shorter days, Halloween, Bonfire Night (UK), Islamic New Year, Thanksgiving, Diwali, St Andrews Day (Scottish)

Winter – cold but cosy, snow and ice, skiing, skating, ice hockey, Hanukkah, Christmas, New Year, Burns' Night (Scottish), Valentine's Day

Spring - new birth, growing plants, St David's Day (Welsh), St Patrick's Day (Irish), Easter, St George's Day (English), the Oscars,

Summer – wedding season, summer holidays, schools closed, vacations, outdoor eating, camping, swimming, keeping cool, Ramadan, Rosh Hashanah

Year round – sports occasions e.g. major events in tennis, golf, football, soccer, car racing, ice hockey, political conventions, elections**, local events and occasions, etc.

And how do these work?

The link between what you want to blog about and the occasion or date can be pretty tenuous – after all, the idea is to catch your readers'/customers' eye with the topical issue as a hook.

If you want to share some short case histories, you might schedule a post for March 17th headlined "St Patrick's Day special: how (YOUR PRODUCT) is helping farmers fight weeds in Ireland"

At the time of one of the major tennis tournaments, you could write "Advantage (YOUR COMPANY): (YOUR SERVICE) at match point to take over lead in (YOUR MARKET)"

In January, (northern hemisphere!) "Icy winter winds blow suppliers' costs down – so we can offer you lower prices on (YOUR PRODUCT)"

In winter, if you have a car-related business … "Snow and ice are pretty, but deadly – here's how to stop your car skating off the road in a skid"

At the time of the Indy 500 or F1 Grand Prix in your country … "Is your business on pole position to win your business race next year?"

A short story that shows how this works

Before the days of blogging when I was specializing in scriptwriting for corporate video etc., I did a hugely successful direct mail campaign to all my clients and prospects at the time of a General Election in the UK.

I sent them each a brightly coloured fabric "election" style rosette with "**Vote For Suze's Scripts**" and my phone number printed at its centre.

Not only did I get a flood of new business in but also more than a year later I would still see those rosettes in pride of place on clients' pin boards. So the seasonal/topical metaphor really does work!

YOU: KEEPING YOUR PERSONALITY

Much as I might bang on about the critical importance of your readers / customers / audience, if it weren't for you, your business blog wouldn't be there.

So in this simple chapter, let's focus on you, the business blog writer extraordinaire.

What do you need to focus on in your business blog writing?

First of all you need to focus on being yourself

This is not always as easy as it sounds, because you don't know personally more than a handful of your readers and the fact that whatever you write in your blog post can, in theory at least, be read by millions of people all over the world.

One way to overcome the rather naked, vulnerable feeling that can generate is to imagine you're writing to one of your readers - one whom you especially like and feel comfortable with. Get yourself in a frame of mind that you would use for an informal talk with this reader, perhaps over some coffee and a sandwich at lunchtime.

Imagine she has asked you to explain and share your thoughts on the topic you want to write about. Decide how you're going to structure your answer so she gets a good grasp of what it's all about, and then talk your way through it. If you want, talk through the structure into a voice recorder and then transcribe it, edit it so you remove all the unnecessary ums, ahs and stumbles. Otherwise write it down as you speak it, give it a final polish and there you go.

That's a written piece of text, blog post, article or whatever else written by you, and that sounds like you.

What if you want to adapt your personality or image for a specific purpose?

Here are some ideas to help you do that without stripping all your own personality out of your text.

If you happen to be a casual, easy-going character who loves to speak in slang, that's great for your personal blog posts, emails, social media etc., but you may feel you want to tidy things up a bit for business.

Change the slang words for slightly more mainstream versions. Although there's nothing wrong with slang provided that it's not offensive, some slang words and phrases have become very tired clichés that make readers groan. Try to think up suitable alternatives and if you're stuck for ideas, use an online thesaurus.

Take out any swear words, but don't lose the sentiment - and equally, don't resort to those rather cheesy "soundalike" versions of common swearing like "darned" instead of "damned," "ruddy" instead of "bloody" and "fricking" instead of "f***ing."

Use your creativity to find the right words

Instead, be a bit creative and find words that express your thought with suitable vehemence but nothing rude. For example, instead of saying "that was a bloody great mistake," say "that was a whopping great mistake" ... or instead of "that was an absolute b*lls-up," say "that was an absolute carve-up."

How about if your normal way of speaking is a bit wordy?

Don't be tempted to try to reduce your rambling while you're talking through the structure of your post - that will cramp your style, as they say. Write it all out verbatim and cut and edit afterwards, leaving in the best parts and remove anything repetitive or superfluous.

What if your natural speaking way is rather shy and nervous?

Don't worry - carry out the structure and speaking exercise as I've described above, and then add to what you've said with a few references, perhaps an example or two, or even a short story that illustrates your points.

In many ways it's easier to expand on your own vocalization than it is to prune it back.

ZERO, STARTING FROM

If you are just starting out with a business blog from zero and are wondering what to write for the first few posts, here are some tips that I found useful when I started HTWB and also a couple of other blogsites I have initiated in the past.

Let's assume that you already know what your blogsite should be all about. What do you need as a basis before you can start attracting readers?

What's a sensible basis for a new business blog launch from zero?

Realistically, before you can start promoting your blogsite so it gets known, you need to have a reasonable number of articles / posts in place so visitors to your new site can have a choice of things to read about.

Despite your blogsite being new, inviting guests to view merely one or two articles inevitably will lead to disappointment on their part which is the last impression you want to leave them with.

How should your posts start out - from scratch?

Obviously you need to write an introductory piece that announces the new blog, and who you are / what your business is. But this does not need to be the first post everyone sees. Why not? Because of the old features versus benefits, "what's in it for me" story.

You may not agree with this and you could well be right, but my feeling is that your first few posts should be real throat-grabbers that address what your (of course!) carefully researched audience is dying to know about.

The introductory information about your new blog can be intertwined in these early posts, and also of course should be written up as an "About" page. But to bring the "all about me/us" story right up front isn't going to get you as many readers, much as it may seem unfair.

What else do you use to "fill up" a brand new blog?

Readers of a new business blog will know damned well that you haven't been collecting "readers' questions" because you've only just started up. But what you can well have been listening to is customers' questions, and these can form very effective bases for early blog posts.

Try to pick the questions that occur most frequently and (dare I say it) if you haven't got enough to hand, you could always make one or two typical questions up. But whatever you do make them real, based on real customers' issues. There's nothing worse than a phony sounding Q&A article.

Most of your readers - existing and potential customers - will appreciate highly relevant "how to" articles.

Obviously the nature of these varies enormously according to your type of business, but invariably there will be some way you can pick up on readers' concerns and give them some easy-to-follow guidelines on processes or other issues.

These articles also have the benefit of letting you write them in bulk, in advance, so that you can load them and schedule them over a period of time.

Industry news and updates are also obvious targets for a new blogsite, but obviously they are time dependent and so you can't upload them in bulk. They make good ongoing articles, though.

Once again, depending on the nature of your business - product and service reviews can help pad out a new blog's content and provide your readers with a new look at that information.

So how much is enough to start out with?

My own view is that you need a bare minimum of 10 articles, if not more. The more the merrier, really.

And much as it is tempting to share your wonderful new business blog with the world at large before you have a significant number of articles/posts settled comfortably in the background, I would resist.

The more you can offer new readers and customers, the more they will like what they read and be sure to come back to your blog for more.

THE END

Well, for now, anyway.

Hope you find this book helpful.

Don't forget to keep checking back to HowToWriteBetter.net for the latest articles, tutorials and other blog writing information.

Happy blogging!

Questions? Give me a shout on suze@suzanstmaur.com

FURTHER READING

HowToWriteBetter.net

My own site …pushing 1,000 free-to-view articles on all types of writing.

Use the search box top right, or the "Categories" drop down menu down on the right-hand side bar.
www.howtowritebetter.net

Wikipedia

Useful for information and quotes but not always accurate
www.en.wikipedia.org

Dictionary.com

Online dictionary and thesaurus, US and UK spellings etc
www.dictionary.reference.com

The Beginner's Guide To SEO, from Moz.com

No BS help to understand and use SEO
www.moz.com/beginners-guide-to-seo

FreeKeywords

Help to find the right keywords for your blogs' SEO

www.freekeywords.wordtracker.com/searches

Google for Wordpress

Shares comments between Google Plus and your WordPress site

www.wordpress.org.support/plugin/sz-google

Social Media Slant

Good site for the latest news in all things social media

www.SocialMediaSlant.com

The BlogMistress

Useful help with anything to do with WordPress blogsites

www.blogmistress.com

Stock.Xchng

Copyright free photos/images

www.sxc.hu

Photo Pin

Copyright free photos/images

www.photopin.com

Law Hound

Online legal services (UK)

www.lawhound.co.uk

Training –N-Promo DIY video

UK workshops on how to shoot and edit good quality video on your smartphone

www.training-n-promo.com

Content curation tools

Swayy

www.swayy.co

Scoop.it

www.scoop.it

Curate.Me

www.curate.me

14 tools and services to stay on top of the news in your industry

www.socialmediaslant.com/news-monitoring-tools/

8 more tools and services to stay on top of the news in your industry

www.socialmediaslant.com/news-monitoring-tools-2/

The Little Big eBook on Social Media Audiences: Build Yours, Keep It, and Win

by Cendrine Marrouat

www.socialmediaslant.com/social-media-audiences

The Little Big eBook on Blogging: 40 Traffic Generation Tips

by Cendrine Marrouat

www.socialmediaslant.com/blogging-ebook

Business Writing Made Easy

by Suzan St Maur

www.howtowritebetter.net – then click on "Suze's Bookshop" top right

Banana Skin Words and how not to slip on them

By Suzan St Maur

www.howtowritebetter.net – then click on "Suze's Bookshop" top right

How To Write Fiction Without The Fuss

By Lucy McCarraher

Available on all Amazons

Get That Job

By Lynn Tulip

www.getthatjobbook.com

ABOUT THE AUTHOR

Canadian-born, UK based Suzan St Maur has written for pretty well every business medium short of tablets of stone (and that only because she's useless with a hammer and chisel).

She now focuses this star-quality experience into blog writing for her clients, plus coaching and training in blog writing for clients who want to write consistently sparkling blog posts for themselves.

She is also a 30+ times published nonfiction author and runs the very popular writing resource, HowToWriteBetter.net - a PR3 grown from nothing to more than 1.5 million page views in just three years, recognized by Alltop.com as one of their top social media sites worldwide.

Suzan lives near Milton Keynes, England with her university student son and numerous dogs and cats.

Made in the USA
Charleston, SC
20 March 2015